INTEGRATING INDIGENOUS COMMUNITIES IN THE MANAGEMENT OF ENVIRONMENTAL RESOURCES IN CAMEROON: A LEGAL APPRAISAL

INTEGRATING INDIGENOUS COMMUNITIES IN THE MANAGEMENT OF ENVIRONMENTAL RESOURCES IN CAMEROON: A LEGAL APPRAISAL

Mbetiji Mbetiji Michel

GALDA VERLAG 2021

Bibliografische Information der Deutschen Nationalbibliothek
Die Deutsche Nationalbibliothek verzeichnet diese Publikation in der Deutschen Nationalbibliografie; detaillierte bibliografische Daten sind im Internet über https://dnb.de abrufbar.

ISBN 978-3-96203-163-3 (Print)
ISBN 978-3-96203-164-0 (E-Book)

FOREWORD

The need to integrate indigenous or local communities in the sustainable management of environmental resources cannot be gainsaid, giving the importance of these resources, as forest to the sustainability of life on the planet. It had been exploited for ages, provides a wide range of benefits, some of which can only be realised if the forest is subjected to limited human intervention. Ecologically forest, serves as the earth's air purifier by reducing the amount of carbon dioxide in the atmosphere during photosynthesis. It is thus a key component in the fight against global warming. Forest, is of great importance to indigenous communities for cultural practices and religious worships. It is certainly for these reasons and others that both the international community and indigenous people are advocating for the integration of indigenous communities in the sustainable management of environmental resources.

This book by Dr. Mbetiji, integrating indigenous communities in the management of environmental resources is of considerable importance. The author is worried that Regional and International Conventions to which Cameroon is a signatory advocate the integration of indigenous communities in the management of environmental resources. Yet these communities are still to become an effective component of the management process.

The land legislation (Ordinance no. 74-1 of 6th July 1974 to establish rules governing land tenure) excludes customary tenure from statutory ownership and militates against community or customary ownership. The abolition of community land and disrespect of customary tenure in Cameroon does not encourage the integration of indigenous communities and the use of indigenous knowledge and practices in the management of natural resources as provided for by Regional and International Conventions. In Papua New Guinea (PNG) on the contrary, forest vests in the customary owners of the land with 97% of the land in that country held under customary tenure. Such a policy serves as an incentive for the participation of indigenous communities in the management of the country's natural resources.

Forests simple management plans (SMPs) focused only on the protection of the tangible values of forests such as timber and non-timber forest product (NTFP) whereas intangible benefits such as ecosystem services equally need to be conserved.

In Cameroon the law requires indigenous communities to form legal entities (Associations, Common Initiative Groups (CIG) Economic Interest Groups (EIG) and Cooperative Societies) to partner with government for the sustainable management of forest resources. These legal entities are financially oriented and their objectives do not tie with sustainable management of forest resources. Membership to legal entities is governed by their articles of association and based on financial requirement which indigenous communities hardly afford. Legal entities are not representatives of indigenous communities because they lack indigenous knowledge and cultural practices needed for the sustainable management of natural resources.

The administrative procedure required for the exploitation of indigenous forest is long, costly, complicated, and fraught with corrupt practices constituting a major drawback for the integration of indigenous communities in the sustainable management of forest resources.

The above state of affairs does not encourage the integration of indigenous communities in the management of natural resources in the country. This calls for an investigation whether indigenous communities are integrated in the management for natural resources following the provisions of International and Regional Conventions, national laws and cultural practices of local communities or they are simply conceptual?

In this book, Dr. Mbetiji highlights the need for government and indigenous communities to work in synergy within the context of integrating local communities in the management of natural resources. The study finds out the nature of indigenous participation and its compatibility with international and national instruments in the sustainable management of natural resources such as forest in the Cameroon. It ascertain that indigenous forest actually exist as required by international conventions and national laws, evaluate their strength, weaknesses and opportunities. In brief the author investigate how in practical terms, implementation and enforcement of integrated natural resource regulations permit indigenous communities to participate in the sustainable management of these resources such as forest in Cameroon.

Given the fact that environmental issues appear to be the biggest issues in the world in term of size, range of problems and skills needed to understand a particular issue, Dr. Mbetiji work can thus not answer all current issues related with the management of environmental resources. The author thus focused on environmental law and specifically on the integration of indigenous people in the management of forest resources which is a component of the environment. There is therefore no doubt that this work will be of relevance not only to persons with legal background, but to humanity as a whole irrespective of background of studies giving the cross disciplinary nature of environmental issues.

Prof. Martha TUMNDE née NJIKAM
Former Deputy Vice-Chancellor in charge of
Internal Control and Evaluation
University of Buea -Cameroon

PREFACE

It has not only been interesting but equally challenging to research on environment law and specifically the integration of indigenous communities in the management of environmental or natural resources such as forest. This is because environmental issues are cross disciplinary and an understanding of any environmental concept requires a basic knowledge of other related disciplines. Indigenous communities have from time immemorial, through the use of customary practices and traditional knowledge been living in harmony with their environment. Colonialism replaced these traditional management systems with technocratic and centralised state management systems which were not only geared towards forest exploitation but also excluding indigenous people from the management of forest resources. After generations of exploitation, the world's forests are in a grim shape and both national and international communities are advocating for the integration of indigenous community in the management of environmental or natural resources. This work therefore investigates how indigenous communities in practical terms, are integrated in the sustainable management of environmental resources such as forest resources in Cameroon.

The book is composed of seven chapters. It opens with a general introduction (Chapter one) in which the historical evolution of participation of indigenous communities in the management of environmental resources is traced. Pre-requisites for the integration of indigenous communities in forest management as well as the services in charged are examined. The chapter equally analyses the characteristics of indigenous forests and ends with the classification of forest in Cameroon to situate the sphere for the integration of indigenous community in the management of forest resources. Chapter two focuses on legislations advocating the integration of indigenous communities in the management of environmental resources. This enabled us to examine how national laws ensure the implementation of the international conventions guaranteeing the integration of local communities in the management of natural resources.

Benefits derived from integrating indigenous communities in the management of environmental resources are examined in chapter three. The chapter classifies these benefits into tangible and intangible and recommends the incorporation of the intangible into Simple Management Plans forests for a better protection of forest ecosystems.

Chapter four focuses on stakeholders promoting the integration of indigenous community in the management of environmental resources. The chapter examines and compares government-created management entities with existing local or indigenous institutions to determine which enhances the integration of local communities in the management of natural resources.

The study of the adverse effects of tenure on the integration of indigenous communities in the management of environmental resources in chapter five clearly shows how the legacy of colonial land administration and forestry legislations reforms negatively affects the integration of indigenous communities in the management of natural resources, as priority is given to statutory tenure without legal recognition of indigenous tenure.

Chapter six examines the encumbrances faced in integrating indigenous communities in the management of natural resources noticeable in incursion of outsiders. Chapter seven presents a summary of the work with recommendations and strategies for effective integration of indigenous communities in the management of natural resources.

This book could not have been accomplished without the contributions of several personalities who I must acknowledge. My gratitude goes first to God Almighty for showering me with His Grace, making it possible for this work to come to fruition.

I am especially thankful to, Prof. Martha TUMNDE née NJIKAM, who despite her challenging academic and administrative duties accepted to proof read this work and to write the forward. I hold in mind, Prof. CHI Augustine MUAM who sacrifices both time and energy to ensure that this book could be completed. Having had a lot of interests and experience in Environmental Law, he provided a lot of literature which facilitated data analyses.

I am thankful to Prof. Cornelius MBIFUNG LAMBI, former Vice Chancellor of the University of Buea and Prof. AMBANASOM Sharack (of Blessed Memory). Though the former is a geographer, he meticulously read part of this book and made substantial correction since environmental issues are multidisciplinary. The latter being a linguist examined the language and corrected the style.

I am also thankful to Prof. NZALIE Joseph, Prof. MBIFI Richard, Prof. DJEUFACK Roland and many others whom I cannot mention because the list is in-exhaustive for the numerous scientific articles they continuously collected for me within and out of the country.

I am lack of words to express my deep appreciation for the altruism and encouragements from my beloved wife SHUMBE NEHMAMFOR Yvonne. Darling, I remain indebted to you for your moral support and the sacrifices you made to see me through during the period of research and writing this book. I cannot end without thanking my children Confidence, Marc-Pride, Miguel, Mivonne and Milton for rendering the environment conducive.

MBETIJI MBETIJI Michel,
The University of Bamenda (UBa),
December 2020.

DEDICATION

To the memory of **MBETIJI Whithney BIHNUI**

TABLE OF CONTENTS

CHAPTER 2: Overview of Legislations Advocating the Integration of Indigenous Communities in the Management of Environmental Resources 13

LIST OF STATUTES

I- Cameroonian

Arrêté no. 00001/MINEP du 03 Février 2007 Définissant le Contenu Général des Termes de référence des Etudes d'Impact Environnemental.

Arrêté no. 0070/MINEP du 22 Avril 2005 Fixant les Différentes catégories d'Opérations dont la Réalisation est Soumise à une Etude d'Impact.

Arrêté Conjoint no. 0520/MINATD/MINFI/MINFOF du 03 Juin 2010 fixant les modalités d'emploi et de suivi de la gestion des revenus provenant de l'exploitation des ressources forestières et fauniques destinés aux communes et aux communautés villageoises riveraines.

Arrêté no. 252/A/CAB/MINEF/DF Portant adoption du modèle de Convention de Gestion des Forêts Communautaires dans le Domaine national.

Décision No. 253/D/MINEF/DF Portant Adoption du Document Intitulé « Manuel de Procédure d'Attribution et des Normes de Gestion des Forêts Communautaires ».

Decree no. 2004/320 of December 8, 2004 relating to the Organisation of Government.

Decree no. 2005/099 of 6th April 2005 Relating to the Organisation of the Ministry of Forestry and Wildlife.

Decree no. 2005/117 relating to the Organisation of the Ministry of Environment and Nature Protection.

Decree no. 2005/481 of 16 December 2005 modifying and completing certain provisions of Decree no. 76/165 of 27th April 1976 to establish the conditions for obtaining land certificates.

Decree no. 2005/495 of December 31, 2005 modifying and completing some provisions of Decree no. 2005/099 of April 6, Relating to the Organisation of the Ministry of Forestry.

Decree no. 76-165 of 27 April 1976 to establish the conditions for obtaining land certificates amended and supplemented by Decree no. 2005-481 of 16 December 2005.

Decree No. 77/245 of July 1977 on the Organisation of Chieftaincy.

Decree no. 92/069 of 9th April 1992 modifying the administrative Structure of Cameroon.

Decree no. 95/413 of 20 June 1995 to determine certain modalities for the application of the fishery regulations.

Decree no. 95/531/PM of 23rd August to determine the conditions for the implementation of the forestry regulations.

Decree no. 95/466/PM of 20 July 1995 to lay down the conditions for the implementation of wildlife regulations.

Décret no. 2005/0577/PM du 23 Février. 2005 Fixant les Modalités de Réalisation des Etudes d'Impact Environnemental.

Law no 96/06 of 18 January 1996 amending the 1972 Constitution of the Republic of Cameroon.

Law no. 81/13 of November 27, 1981 to lay down Forestry, Wildlife and Fisheries Regulations

Law no. 90/53 of 19 December 1990 on Freedom of Associations.

Law no. 92/006 of 14 August 1992 on Co-operative and Common Initiative Groups.

Law no. 93/015 of 12 December 1993 on Economic Interest Groups.

Law no. 94/01 of 20th January 1994 to lay down Forestry Wildlife and Fisheries Regulations.

Law no. 96/12 of August 5, 1996 Relating to Environment Management.

Ordinance no. 74/1 of July 6, 1974 to establish rules governing land tenure.

Lettre Circulaire no. 0655/LC/MINFOF/SG/DF relative à la mise en application des instructions générales permettant à déterminer l'origine et la Tracabilité des produits forestiers circulant sur le territoire national

Ordinance no. 74/2 of 6 July 1974 to establish rule governing State lands.

Southern Cameroon's High Court Law 1955.

II- Foreign Statutes

Benin, *Loi no. 93-009 du Juillet 1993 portant Régime des Forêt.*

Congo Kinshasa, *Projet de loi Forestière Août 2000.*

DRC, *Loi no. 011/2002 Portant Code Forestier.*

Gabon, *loi no. 16/01/2001 du 31/11/2001 portant Code Forestier.*

Guinea, *Loi no. l/99/013 du 22 Juin 1999 adoptant et promulguant la Loi portant Code Forestier.*

Guinea-Bissau, 1991 Forestry Law.

Niger, 1999 Forestry Bill.

Nigeria, Evidence Ordinance Cap 62, 1958.

Rwanda, *Loi no. 74/1988 du 5 Décembre 1988 portant Organisation du Régime Forestier.*

Senegal, *Décret 98-164 du 20 Février 1999 portant Code Forestier.*

Senegal, *Loi 98-03 du 18 Janvier 1998, Portant Code Forestier.*

Togo, *Projet de loi portant Code des Ressources Forestières, 1998.*

III- International Instruments

African Charter on Human and Peoples' Rights (1986)

African Convention on Nature and Natural Resources (1968)

COMIFAC Treaty (2005)

Convention Concerning the Protection of the World Cultural and Natural Heritage (1972)

International Covenant on Civil and Political Rights (1966)

International Covenant on Economic, Social and Cultural Rights (1966)

International Labour Organisation (ILO) Convention 169

Maputo Convention on Nature and Natural Resources (2003)

Non-Legally Binding Authoritative Statement of Principles for a Global Consensus on the Management, Conservation and Sustainable Development of all Types of Forests (Forest Principles) (1992).

OHADA Uniform Act on Commercial Companies and Economic Interest Groups (1998)

OHADA Uniform Act securities (1997)

Protocol on Substances that deplete the Ozone Layer, Montreal (1987)

Rio Declaration on Environment and Development (1992)

Statutes of the I. C. J.

Stockholm Declaration on Human Environment (1972)

UN Convention on the Elimination of All Form of Racial Discrimination (1969)

UN Convention on the Rights of the Child (1989)

UN Convention to Combat Desertification (UNCCD) (1994)

UN Declaration on the Rights of Indigenous People (2007)

UN Convention on Biological Diversity (1992)

UN Framework Convention on climate change (1992)

UN General Assembly Resolution A/RES/54/214

UN General Assembly Resolution 61/295

Vienna Convention on the Law of Treaties (1969)

LIST OF CASES

I- Cameroonian Cases

Alexander Duru V. Haddison Masalo, [1948] CASWP/CC/52/80.

Amidou Lukong V. Razel Road Construction Company Ltd. HCK/5/95 (unreported).

Chief Lobe Njembele v. Benedict Nsombai (1980) CASWP/20/70 Unreported

Chritopher v. Anye Henry Saningong Appeal no. BCA/7cc/92 (unreported)

Egbe Boardman v. Bimbia Bonadikombo Community Forest, Suit no. LM/100/05-06 (unreported)

Enjema Liote v. Hannah Forty [1948] CASWP/CC/15/82

Immaculate Wanga Vefonge v. Samuel Lyonga Yukpe (1981) CASWP/CC/25/81 (unreported).

Kimbi Moses Ndoh v. Groupement D'Entreprise Trapp-Strabag Belfinger + Berger, WHC/2/98 (unreported)

Laikom Community Forest Management Group v. Ngam Samson and other, Suit no. CFIF/0/M/02-0

Ndange v. Ngeh (1975) BCA/16/74 (unreported)

Ndefru Zama Odilia, Tumanjong Nanga, & Tawah Mary v. Che Fongwa John (1998) BCA/3/98 (unreported)

Ngeh v. Ngome (1962-64) WCLR 321.

Presbyterian Church moderator v. D.C Johnny, (1974) BCA/27/74, unreported.

The People v. Isaiah Mangeh & 138 Ors (2003) (unreported), BCA/35/2002 delivered on 16 July 2003.

II- Foreign Cases

Amodu Tijani v. Secretary Southern Nigeria [1921] 2 AC 399.

Calder v. Attorney General of British Columbia [1973] 34 DLR (3d) 145, at 190.

Conseil d'Etat 31 Juillet 1912, Société des Granits Porphyroides des Vosges.

Conseil d'Etat 20 Avril 1956, Epoux Bertin et Ministre de l'Agriculture c. Consorts Grimouard.

Delgamuukw v. British Columbia. [1997] 3 S.C.R, 1010, 1082.

Eshugbayi v. Nigerian Government (1931) AC 662.

Lancaster v. Eve (1859)141 E.R. 288 at 293.

Mabo v. Queensland (no 2) (1992) 66 ALJR 408, at 146.

R v. Symonds (1847) NZPCC 387 (SC (NZ), at 390.

Ramsden v. Dyson (1866) L.R.H.C. 129.

United State v. Shoshone Tribe of Indians 304 US 111 (1938) WHC/2/98 (unreported).

Wik Peoples v. Queensland & Ors [1997] 187 CLR 1, at 84.

Wolverhampon and Walsall Railway Co v. London and Northern Railway Co (1873) LR 16 Eq 433 at 439.

Wuta-Ofei v. Danguah (1961) 1 WLR 1238 at 1243

LIST OF ABBREVIATIONS

Art.	:	Article
ATEM	:	ATOTENA de MEBEM
BBNRMC	:	Bimbia Bonadikombo Natural Resource Management Council
BHFP	:	Bamenda Highland Forest Project
BOPO	:	Boomaboong and Pouth-Njock
CADBAP	:	Communauté Active pour le Déveoppement des Bakoum, Baka et Pol
CAID	:	Canadian Agency for International Develpoment
CBD	:	Convention on Biological Diversity
CED	:	Centre Pour L'Environnment et le Développement
CEFDHAC	:	Conférence Sur les Ecosystèmes des Forêts Denses et Humides D'Afrique Centrale
CEMAC	:	Economic and Monetary Community of Central Africa
CF	:	Community Forest
CFDP	:	Community forestry Development Project
CFN	:	Community Forestry Network
CFU	:	Community Forest Unit
CFUG	:	Community Forest User Groups
CIEFE	:	Centre International d'Etudes Forestière et Environnementale
CIFOR	:	Centre for International Forestry Research
CIG	:	Common Initiative Group
CITES	:	Convention on International Trade in Endangered Wildlife Species
CO.PA.L	:	Coopérative des Planteurs de la Lékié

CO2	:	Carbon Dioxide
COFAYET	:	Forêt Communautaire Andoꞌo Yetsang
DACEFI	:	Développement Alternative Communautaire a Lꞌexploitation Forestière Illégale
DFID	:	British Department for International Development
DIDILO	:	DIPAN DI LONG
DO	:	Divisional Officer
DRC	:	Democratic Republic of Congo
Ed	:	Editor
Edit	:	Edition
EIG	:	Economic Interest Group
Et al	:	And Others
FAO	:	Food and Agricultural Organization
FASA	:	Faculty of Agronomy and Agricultural Sciences
FCFA	:	Francs de la Communauté Financière Africaine
FMO	:	Forest Management Officer
FOVYVE	:	Forces Vives Yembani Vela
FTP	:	Forests Trees and People
FTPP	:	Forest Trees and People Programme
GBOPABA	:	Ngola Community Forest management Association representing the Gbo, Pâ and Bamouh communities of Ngola and Achip
GROPAM	:	Groupe d'Initiative Commune des Agriculteurs de Minkoe- Mbogo
GIC	:	Groupe D'Initiative Commune
GICAM	:	Groupe d'Initiative Commune des Agriculteur de Ngam II"
HRC	:	Human Right Commission
Ibid	:	Ibidem (in the same place, book or source)
ICCPR	:	International Convention on Civil and Political Rights

ICESCR	:	International Covenant on Economic, Social and Cultural Rights
IIED	:	International Institute for Environment and Development
ILO	:	International Labour Organisation
IMF	:	International Monetary Fund
IMPM	:	Institution of Medical Research and Medicinal Plants Studies
IRAD	:	Institution of Agronomic Research and Development
JAGRA	:	Jeunes Agriculteurs D'Andjouk
MA	:	Management Agreement
MINADER	:	Ministry of Agriculture and Rural Development
MINATD	:	Ministry of Territorial Administration and Decentralisation
MINFI	:	Ministry of Finance
MINEF	:	Ministry of Environment and Forestry
MINEPDED	:	Ministry of Environment and Nature Protection and Sustainable development
MINFOF	:	Ministry of Forestry and Wildlife
MINRESI	:	Ministry of Scientific Research and Innovation
MINESUP	:	Ministry of Higher Education
NDECUDA	:	Ndissi-Ekeb Cultural and Development Association
NGO	:	Non- Governmental Organization
NRI	:	Natural Resource Institute
NTFP	:	Non Timber Forest Products
NWFP	:	Non Wood Forest Products
ODA	:	Overseas Development Association
OFI	:	Oxford Forestry Institute
OHADA	:	Organisation pour L'Harmonisation en Afrique du Droit des Affaires

ONADEF	:	Office National de Dévelopment des forêts
OUP	:	Oxford University Press,
PFPF	:	Partners for Productivity Foundation
PERAD	:	Protection de L'Environnement, Recherche et Appui au Développement
PIP	:	Public Information Programme
PNG	:	Papua New Guinea
PNUD	:	Programme des Nations Unies pour le Développement
REDD	:	Reducing Emission from Deforestation and forest Degradation
REPA	:	Rural Environmental Poverty and Alleviation
RIGC	:	Projet de Renforcement des Initiatives pour la Gestion Communautaire des Ressources Forestières et Fauniques
SNV	:	Nertherlands Development Organisation
SCHCL	:	Southern Cameroons High Court Law
SDO	:	Senior Divisional Officer
Sect	:	Section
SMP	:	Simple Management Plan
TCC-CIG	:	Tinto clan community forest
UA	:	Uniform Act
UK	:	United Kingdom
UNEP	:	United Nations Environmental Programme
UN	:	United Nations
USAID	:	United States Agency for International Development
VDC	:	Village Development Committees
WBEP	:	World Bank Environmental Paper
WHC	:	World Heritage Convention
WNH	:	World Natural Heritage

CHAPTER ONE

INTRODUCTION OVERVIEW

1.1: Pressure for Integrated Natural Resource Management

Before colonialism, indigenous communities in Africa were living in harmony with their environment. Colonialism replaced traditional management systems with technocratic and centralised state management systems which were principally geared towards forest exploitation since priority was given to trees at the expense of the people who used them.[1] Hence, in some countries Governments awarded lucrative forest concessions to political allies without considering the needs of indigenous communities and the ecological functions of forest. Forest was seen as a source of capital for political control and not as a resource worth preserving.[2]

After generations of exploitation, the world's forests are in a grim shape. Out of the 3.45 billion hectares (1/3) of the earth's surface covered by forest, about 15-17 million hectares are lost yearly.[3] Cameroon has lost about 60% of its forest.[4] At this rate very few forests will survive and such massive forest loss threatens the existence of local communities who depend on non-timber forest products (NTFP) for subsistence; and the world at large since forests serve as major carbon sinks for mitigating the adverse effects of climate change.

---

[1] Dubois, O., "Rights and Wrongs of Rights to Land and Forest Resources in Sub-Saharan Africa. Bridging the Gap between Customary and Formal Rules," IIED Available at www.oneworld.org/iied (last consulted 10/01/2011).

[2] This was for instance the case in the Philippines, where under President Ferdinand Marcos, forest was treated as a resource to be dilapidated. http://www.american.edu/TED/philwood.htm (last consulted 26/12/2011).

[3] BHFP, Community Forestry Seminar Series. Information note no. 1: The importance of the forest of the North-West, their biodiversity conservation and value to local communities, October 2001.

[4] USAID, Cameroon's Natural Resource Management Assessment, IRG, Washington, 1991, p. 14.

To prevent this deplorable situation, International and Regional Conventions ratified by Cameroon have for long advocated the participation of local communities, endowed with indigenous knowledge in the sustainable management of forests. Agitation by local communities to be involved in the management of forest resources left Government with no choice than to respect international Conventions to involve local communities in forest management.

1.1.1: Influence of International Conventions

International Conventions are at forefront in the fight to have local or indigenous communities involved in the management of their forest. Prominent amongst these Conventions is the 1992 United Nations Convention on Biological Diversity (CBD). The Convention states that environmental issues are best handled when all citizens are given the opportunity to participate in decision-making processes and calls on contracting states to:

> ... respect, preserve and maintain knowledge, innovations and practices of indigenous and local communities embodying traditional lifestyles relevant for the conservation and sustainable use of biological diversity and promote their wider application with the approval and involvement of the holders of such knowledge, innovations and practices and encourage the equitable sharing of the benefits arising from the utilization of such knowledge, innovations and practices.[5]

Similar provisions are found in other instruments stressing the participation of local/ indigenous communities in the sustainable management of environmental resources. Examples are principle 22 of the 1992 Rio Declaration, which provides that:

> Indigenous people and their communities and other local communities have a vital role in environmental management and development because of their knowledge and traditional practices. States should recognize and duly support

[5] Article 8 (j) of 1992 CBD.

> their identity, culture and interests and enable their effective participation in the achievement of sustainable development.

Article 6 (a) (iii) of the 1992 UN Convention on Climate Change calls on "states to promote and facilitate public participation in addressing climate change and its effects". Article xvii (3) of the 2003 Maputo Convention on Nature and Natural Resources stipulates that:

> … parties shall take the measures necessary to enable active participation by the local communities in the process of planning and management of natural resources upon which such communities depend with a view of creating local incentives for the conservation and sustainable use of such resources.

The 1992 Non-Legally Binding Authoritative Statement of Principles for a Global Consensus on the Management, Conservation and Sustainable Development of all Types of Forests (Forest Principles) is also illustrative. Article 2 (d) of the Forest Principles provides that:

> Governments should promote and provide opportunities for the participation of interested parties, including local communities and indigenous people, industries, … non-governmental organizations and individuals, forest dwellers and women, in the development, implementation and planning of national forest policies.

Within the Central African Sub-Region the 1996 *Conférence Sur les Ecosystèmes des Forêts Denses et Humides D'Afrique Centrale* (CEFDHAC) and the Yaounde Declaration of March 1999 emphasized the need for countries in the Congo Basin to manage forest resources with the participation of local communities. The 1999 Yaounde Declaration culminated in the 2005 COMIFAC Treaty which calls on member states to:

> Step up efforts to increase the rapid participation of rural populations in the planning and sustainable

> management of ecosystems and allot adequate areas for their socio-economic development.[6]

Other stakeholders in advocating the participation of indigenous communities in forest management are international donor Organizations such as the International Monetary Fund (I.M.F), the World Bank, Food and Agricultural Organization (FAO). They make promises of material and financial assistance to states that adopt policies that involve local communities and promote their active participation in forest management.[7]

The multiplicity of international obligations advocating the participation of local communities in the management of environmental resources is evidence of the weaknesses of state management systems and acknowledgment of the need of local communities, the use of indigenous knowledge and cultural practices in the management of natural resources.

1.1.2: The Intervention of Indigenous Communities

Featuring among poor countries where most inhabitants directly depend on natural environment to survive and progress,[8] Cameroon like other African countries experienced poverty and hardship following changes in foreign trade balances in the early 1990s.[9] This hardship was attributed to the drop in oil prices whereby oil lost about 24% of its value,[10] and the devaluation of the FCFA in 1994[11] reducing the purchasing power of local communities. The economic crisis caused mass redundancy in the public and private sectors, causing many people to turn to farming, thus clearing forests for firewood and subsistence agriculture. Organised illegal fuel wood merchants destroyed forest reserves by felling trees to supply the markets with firewood,[12] leading to forest degradation.

---

[6] Article 1 of the 2005 Treaty on the conservation and sustainable management of forest ecosystems in Central Africa and to establish the Central African Forests Commission (COMIFAC).

[7] Hazell, P and Magrath, W., "Summary of World Bank Forestry Paper," in Cleaver, K. et al., (eds) Conservation of West and Central African Rainforest, WBEP, no 1, Washington D.C USA, 1992, p. 16.

[8] Lescuyer, G. L et al., Forest Law Enforcement and Rural Livelihoods: A (Socio- economic) Case Study in Cameroon, CIFOR, Yaounde, 2003, p. 5.

[9] Manga, B. E., "Cameroon's Biodiversity Conservation Policy: The Case of the Mount Cameroon Project," A Doctoral (3ème cycle) thesis, IRIC, Yaounde, 2000, p. 57.

[10] Ibid.

[11] Burnley, G. E., "The Role of Women in the Promotion of Forest Products," in Non-Wood Forest Products of Central Africa. Current Research Issues and Prospects for Conservation and Development, F.A.O, 1999, p. 139.

[12] Ibid.

Witnessing the disappearance of "their forests," associated with traditional, social, spiritual and local economic values, some communities could not stay indifferent. They took upon themselves to protect "their forests" against illegal activities, although with very minimal impact in redressing forest degradation resulting from fire and excessive firewood collection.[13] Communities began calling for the return of "their forests" and the rights to manage them.

The demand of indigenous communities to take control and manage forest resources is not peculiar to Cameroon. In Nepal and India the participation of local communities in the management of forest resources was as a result of pressure from local communities themselves to manage these resources.[14] In Nepal the nationalisation of forest land in 1957 led to rapid forest degradation and the country lost a large percentage of it forest land in the 1960s and 70s. Acknowledging the weaknesses of state management and the demand from local communities to manage forest, a series of legislation were enacted giving local communities control of forest resources and priority over other potential users of the forest lands.[15]

Joint Forest Management (JFM) in India is a result of local communities claiming rights to forest, and a recognition that forests were being degraded under state management regime. This is certainly the reason why JFM is principally focused on reforestation and sustainable management of degraded forest land.[16] In Guatemala, pressure for local communities to manage forest resources was exerted by International Conservation Organisations and the United States Agency for International Development (USAID).[17]

To meet the exigencies of Regional and International Conventions, coupled with pressures from local communities to manage forests, a good number of African countries were constrained to associate indigenous communities in the management of forest and other natural resources.

---

13 Bojang F., "Overview of International Workshop on Community Forestry in Africa" in Proceedings of International Workshop on Community Forestry in Africa, 1999, p. 8.

14 Long, C., Forest and Community control: Official process that permits formal recognition of community management and rights and their relevance to the Democratic Republic of Congo, IIED, 2010, p. 10 &17.

15 Ibid p. 10.

16 Ibid p. 17.

17 Ibid p. 22.

The initiatives took the form of legislative reforms in the forests sector, resulting either in the drafting and adoption of new laws, amendment of existing ones,[18] or making public declaration to that effect.[19] These laws strengthened and legally recognised indigenous communities as partners in the management of forest and related resources.

The notion of integrating indigenous people in forests management thus emerged with many synonyms or models such as Joint Forest Management in India, Collaborative Forest Management in England, Co-management of Forest in Peru, and Social Forestry[20] all aimed at enhancing the level of local communities' participation in forest management.

The participation of indigenous communities in the management of the world's forest has therefore been increasing since the last 25 years and the forest area under local community management is approaching 25% globally.[21] Indigenous / community forests are implemented in about 35 African countries with 20 countries having enabling policy framework in place.[22]

---

[18] Examples are:

- Senegal, *Loi no. 98-03 du 18 Janvier 1998 portant Code Forestière* (section R. 9 recognises the rights of local communities to manage forests)
- Rwanda, *Loi no. 74/1988 du 5 Décembre 1988 portant Organisation du Régime Forestier* (Article 51-60 gives the possibility to local communities to manage forests)
- Benin, *Loi no. 93-009 du Juillet 1993 portant Régime des Forêt.* (Article 44 introduces forest management agreement that can be signed between local communities and the forestry administration.)
- Guinea, *Loi no. l/99/013 du 22 Juin 1999 adoptant et promulguant la Loi portant Code Forestier* (Article 42 recognised forest land belonging to decentralised authorities) and
- Cameroon, Law no. 94/01 f 20th January 1994 to lay down Forestry Wildlife and Fisheries Regulations (section 30-33, and 37 provides for councils and community forests)

[19] During the Summit of Central African Heads of States on the conservation of the tropical forests held in Yaounde, March 1999, President Paul Biya reaffirmed his resolution to encourage the involvement of local communities in the management of forest resources of which they are custodians. Cf. Speech of the Minister of Forestry and Wildlife, Mr. Sylvester NAAH ONDOA during the Official Launching of the Community Forest Public Information Programme in Cameroon, DFID, MINEF, Yaounde Conference Centre 29-30 November 1999.

[20] Chimere, M. D et Oyono P. R., « Instrumentalités et Déficit des Intineraires de Décentralisation de la Gestion des Ressources Naturelles au Cameroun » in Bulletin Arbres, Forêts et Communautés Rurales, no. 15/16, Spécial Cameroun, 1998, p. 20. This opinion is equally shared by Fisher, R. J., Cogestion des Forêts pour le Conservation et le Développement WWF, UICN, France, 1995, pp. 2&5.

[21] Schreckenberg, K et al., "Participatory forest management. An overview," March 2006. Available at http//www.fao.org/forestry/foris/webview/forestry2/index.jsp (Last consulted on 11/06/2011).

[22] Barrow, E et al., "Customary Practices and Forest Tenure Reforms in Africa- Status, Issues and lessons" in Rights and Resources Initiatives. A Global Coalition to Advance Forest Tenure, Policies and Market Reforms, CIFOR, 2009, p. 6.

1.2: Pre-Requisites for the Integration of Indigenous Communities in the Management of Natural Resources

Community forest, which reflects people's participation,[23] motivates local communities to mobilise rural resources and capacities, thus become active rather than passive subjects, manage resources, make decisions and control activities that affect their live.[24] The Forestry Law defines community forest as "a forest of the non-permanent state forest, object of a management agreement between a village community and the services in charge of forestry[25] or government. Three elements (community, forest and government) are highlighted.

1.2.1: Community

A community is important in this context in the creation and management of forest resources because as the name suggest, without community, we cannot talk of community forests. A community could be considered as a group of people residing together and bound by agreed norms and values.[26] In Mozambique a community is defined as being no larger than the population or area of a locality while in Scotland a community consist of not more than 10.000 people.[27] In Cameroon there is no limit to the size of a community and in our context can refer to a group residing close to the forest that depends on it for subsistence and livelihood.

1.2.2: Forest

The Cameroon forestry law defines it as any land covered by vegetation with the predominance of trees, shrubs and other species capable of providing products other than agricultural produce.[28] It includes wildlife which means all species belonging to any natural ecosystem as well as animal species captured from their natural habitat for domestication

---

[23] Sten Hagberg., "Management of Natural Forests. The Gazetted Forest Reserve of Toumousséni, Burkina Faso," FTP, Uppsala, 1992, (this document is not paginated).

[24] Well, M. et al., People and Parks, Linking Protected Area Management with Local Communities, WB,WWF,USAID, Washington DC, 1999, p. 42.

[25] Article 3 (11) of Decree no. 95/531/PM of 23rd August to determine the conditions for the implementation of the forestry regulations.

[26] For more on the definition of community see, FAO, Common Forest Resource Management. Annoted Bibliography of Asia, Africa, and Latin America. FTP-FAO, Rome, 1993, p. 8.

[27] Long (n 14) 20.

[28] Section 2 of the 1994 Forestry Law.

purpose to constitute part of the forest.[29] Forest is equally defined by FAO as "land with a tree canopy cover of more than 10% and area of more than 0.5 hectares and a minimum tree height of 5 meters.[30] Indigenous or community forest has the above characteristics.

1.2.3: Service in charge of Forestry or Government

The government is represented by the service in charge of forestry which in Cameroon is the Ministry of Forestry and Wildlife headed by a Minister. The structure of this Ministry provides for a Sub-Directorate of community forest with the following functions:

- Implementation of state policies related to community forests;
- Follow-up development of community forests and ensures community forest data-base;
- Up-date the Manual of Procedure and Norms for the Management of community forests;
- Approve Simple Management Plans of community forests;
- Ensure the respect of procedure in the attribution and management of community forests;
- Elaborates, coordinates and supervises sensitisation and training programmes on laws governing community forests.[31]

The Sub-Directorate of community forest is represented at the local level by Regional and Divisional services of Forestry and Wildlife, which oversee the creation or designation and management of community forests.

1.3: Characteristics of Indigenous Forest Management

Local communities will be encouraged to participate in the sustainable management of community forests if the following attributes are respected.

1.3.1: Benefit sharing

Without equitable sharing of benefits, local communities will not be motivated to participate in the management of community forests. That

---

[29] Ibid, section 3.

[30] UNEP, African Environmental Outlook; Past Present and Future Perspectives, 2002, p. 130.

[31] Article 36 of Decree no. 2005/099 of 6th April Relating to the Organisation of the Ministry of Forestry and Wildlife.

is why the 1992 CBD, provides for "equitable sharing of benefits arising out of the utilization of genetic resources."[32]

In keeping with this requirement, the law provides that all the revenue (100%) derived from community forests belong entirely to the community concerned and is managed by the community forest legal entity in conformity with its simple management plan (SMP). The law further stipulates that a maximum of 10% of the revenue should be used for running the community forest legal entity while a minimum of 90% be used for the realization of projects previewed in the community forest SMP.[33]

1.3.2: Equity

Equity here should be understood in the broad sense of the word which is what is good, just and honest in human transaction and not in its narrow technical sense.[34] This requires honesty and transparency in all transactions, hence the need to enforce the provisions of community forest management agreements in good faith. Equity implies the respect of international conventions advocating the participation of local communities in the management of natural resources based on the principle of *pacta sunt servanda* which states that "every treaty in force is binding upon the parties to it and must be performed by them in good faith."[35]

1.3.3: Flexibility

Flexibility here should be regarded as the ability of the various stakeholders to adapt and respond to changing situations. For instance, the forestry administration which has the role of keeping watch over the management of community forest should promote and adopt indigenous management practices that are compatible with sustainable forest management as exits in Nepal and Gambia,[36] and recommended by International Law. For instance the 1992 CBD obliges contracting Parties to:

---

[32] Article 1 of the 1992 CBD.

[33] See articles 6 and 22 (2) of *Arrête Conjoint no. 0520/MINATD/MINFI/MINFOF du 03 Juin 2010 fixant les modalités d'emploi et de suivi de la gestion des revenues provenant de l'exploitation des ressources forestières et fauniques destines aux communes et aux communautés villageoises riveraines.*

[34] Equity in the narrow technical sense refers to the body of rules which were formulated and applicable by the English Court of Chancery before the advent of the Judicature Act 1873-75. For more on this see Halliwell, M., Equity and Trust, Old Bailey Press, 2nd edit., London, 2000.

[35] See article 26 of the 1969 Vienna Convention on the Law of Treaties.

[36] Long (n 14) 20.

Respect preserve and maintain knowledge, innovations and practices of indigenous and local communities embodying traditional lifestyles relevant for the conservation and sustainable use of biological diversity.[37]

1.3.4: Local rights

Customary rights of local communities should be respected, because of the ecological, economic, social, and cultural values of the forest to the communities concerned. Unless such rights are recognised and protected local communities will not be motivated to participate in the sustainable management of forest.

1.3.5: Sustainability

One of the reasons for the creation of a community forest is to enhance sustainable management of forest. The concept of sustainable management is stated in article 2 of the 1992 CBD as the use of biological resources in a way and at a rate that does not lead to long term decline of biological diversity, thereby maintaining it potentials to meet the needs and aspirations of present and future generations. Explicit reference is made to sustainability, in almost all forestry texts within the African continent, where participation of local communities in the management of such resources is envisaged.[38]

1.4: The Classification of Forests

Before 1994, national forest estate was classified as State forests; Council forests; Private forests; and Communal forests,[39] offering no

---

[37] See article 8 (j) of the 1992 CBD.

[38] The following are illustrative:
- In Senegal, Section R.11 of "Décret 98-164 du 20 Février 1999 portant Code Forestière, partie réglementaire" requires forest management to take into consideration ecological and socio-economic conditions of the area concerned.
- In Niger section 10 of the Forestry Bill of 1999 states that national forestry policy must be based on the principle of sustainability.
- In Togo, section 2 of "Projet de loi portant Code des Ressources Forestières, Novembre 1998", provides that the protection and development of forest resources are to be guaranteed through sustainable methods to meet the present and future needs while contributing to the conservation of the environment and biodiversity.
- See also Section 1 of Projet de loi Forestière Août 2000 of Congo Kinshasa; Section 26 of Benin "Décret 96271 du 2 Juillet 1996 portant modalités d'application de la loi 93-009 du 2 Juillet 1993. All these laws make references to sustainability in the management of forest resources.

[39] Article 2 of Law no. 81/13 of 27 November 1981 to lay down Forestry, Wildlife and Fisheries Regulations.

opportunity for local communities to participate in the management of forest resources. Today, as previewed by the 1994 Forestry Law, the national forest estate is divided into two main categories, composed of permanent and non-permanent forests.[40]

Permanent forests are forests found on permanent forestland, which is land used solely for forestry and wildlife habitat. Permanent forest represents the country's ecological diversity and is intended to cover at least 30% of the total area of the national territory,[41] and consist of State and Council forests which are not within the scope of this work.

Non-permanent or unclassified forests are forests on non-permanent forestland, which is land that may be used for other purposes other than forestry. This category is made up of communal forests, forests belonging to private individuals and community forests.

[40] Section 20 of the 1994 Forestry Law.
[41] Ibid section 22.

CHAPTER TWO

OVERVIEW OF LEGISLATIONS ADVOCATING THE INTEGRATION OF INDIGENOUS COMMUNITIES IN THE MANAGEMENT OF ENVIRONMENTAL RESOURCES

2.1: Introduction

Cameroon has one of the largest reserves of rainforests left in the world, which it shares with neighbouring countries of the Congo basin[42] (Congo, Gabon, Equitorial Guinea, The Democratic Republic of Congo, and Central African Republic). The legal framework instituted by colonial powers for the management of forest resources has evolved and has been amended and reinforced by both local and international legislation since independence in 1960.[43] An examination of legal and institutional frameworks put in place for the implementation and enforcement of international engagements such as the 1992 Convention on Biological Diversity (CBD) which recommended for the participation of local communities in the management of forest resources is within the scope of this chapter. A review of relevant laws in some countries of the Congo Basin is also made, given the trans-boundary nature of forests in countries in Central Africa.

---

[42] www.pbs.org/.../africa/...reainforest/rainforest_overview_lo.html. (Last consulted on 3/3/11); See also Besong, J and Ngwasiri, C. N., "The 1994 Forestry Law and Rational Resource Management in Cameroon," A PVO-NGO/NRMS Cameron publication, Yaounde, 1995, p. 3.

[43] French (East) Cameroon achieved independence in 1960 while British (West) Cameroon achieved its own independence by joining French "Cameroun" in 1961. For more on this see Mbuagbaw, T. Y et al., A History of the Cameroon, New Edit, Longman, 1988, p. 118.

2.2: Indigenous/ community Forests-oriented Instruments

The involvement of Cameroon in the preservation of natural resources at least statutorily could be traced from the colonial era. The Germans enacted the first Forestry Ordinance in Cameroon on the 4th of April 1900.[44] This Ordinance required the Governor to compel illegal harvesters of timber to replace the trees felled. The Ordinance equally enjoined the Governor to take measures to plant the trees at the cost of the defaulters if necessary by distraining their properties.

The 1900 Imperial Forestry Ordinance was followed by an Ordinance in 1913 which regulated the harvesting of forest products from crown land and native reserves.[45] Paragraph 1 empowered Government or those to whom the Governor granted the rights to harvest forest products on crown land and those parts of native reserves, yet to be put at the disposal of the natives. Through this Ordinance, the German administration took control of all forest resources in Kamerun, today Cameroon, a policy which till date reverberates in Cameroon's current Forestry Law. For instance section 39 (4) of the 1994 Forestry Law stipulates that:

> Forest products ...found in natural forests on land belonging to a private individual shall be the property of the State, except where the said products have been acquired by the person concerned in accordance with the laws and regulations in force.

With the defeat of the Germans in 1916 during the First World War,[46] Cameroon was partitioned between Britain and France and administered under the League of Nations mandate system. This partition was confirmed by an agreement signed in London on July 10, 1919 and later by the Council of the League of Nations on July 20, 1922.[47]

---

[44] Ngwasiri, C. N et al., "Legislative and Institutional Instruments for the Sustainable Management of Non- Timber Forest Products (NTFP) in Cameroon, Past, Present and Unresolved Issues," C.F.D.P, October 2002, p. 9.

[45] Tumnde, M. S., "Integrating Law and Local Customs in Forest Resource Management around the Mount Cameroon Region," in Lambi, C. M., and Eze, E. B., (eds.) Reading in Geography, UPCA, Bamenda Cameroon, 2001, p. 356.

[46] This was from 1915-1919. For more on this, see Mbuagbaw, T. Y et al., A History of the Cameroon. New Edit, Longman, 1988 p. 78.

[47] Tumnde (n 4) 357.

The first British Forestry Ordinance applicable in British Cameroon was the Forestry Ordinance of 4th March 1916 which was enacted before the confirmation of the British mandate. Its application was guaranteed by Section 9 of the mandate agreement which provided that:

> The Mandatory shall have full powers of administration and legislation in the areas subject to the mandate. The area shall be administered in accordance with the laws of the Mandatory as an integral part of his territory... The Mandatory shall therefore be at liberty to apply his laws to the territory under the Mandate subject to the modification required by local conditions...

Section 4 of the 1916 Ordinance gave the Governor wide powers to ensure the conservation of forests. The Governor could constitute as reserve any government land, native land and land on which forest destruction was negatively affecting water supply or affecting the continuous supply of forest products to the village communities and the environs. This Ordinance empowered the Governor to control the use and management of forest resources. It conferred on him discretionary powers to constitute forest reserves from which individual rights could be alienated. For instance failure to exercise the rights to harvest forest products or graze cattle in a reserve for ten years justified extinction of those rights.[48] The Governor equally made regulations controlling the harvesting of forest products on both government and native lands and prohibited any class of persons specified in his regulations from marketing forest products both locally and internationally.[49]

This Ordinance underwent several amendments before and after independence.[50] These amendments were aimed at reinforcing State authority to dispose of, and regulate the use of the forest.[51] They limited the influence of local communities in forest management, and are responsible for the poor management of community forests today as will be seen later.

---

48 Tumnde (n 4) 357.

49 Ibid.

50 Ibid. See also, Funwie, T. C., 'Community Forest Management Entities as Effective Tools for Local-Level Participation under Cameroonian Law: Case Study of Kilum/Ijim Mountain Forest." A Ph.D Thesis, University of Yaounde II, September 2007, p. 79 who talks of amendments in 1927, 1935, 1948 and 1965.

51 cf. Funwie (n 9).

The French administration in French Cameroon issued a Decree on Forestry in 1922 with the objective of regulating forest exploitation. This was followed four years later by a more comprehensive forest regulation embedded in a Decree issued on March 8, 1926. This classified all forests in the country as *Forêts domaniales* and placed them under the authority of the High Commissioner, conferring on him powers to allocate up to 10.000 hectares of forestland.[52] Indigenous people were granted continuous enjoyment of their rights of usage over wood and other forest products, as well as over hunting. They were prohibited from exploitation of forest resources for commercial purposes with the exception of palm trees. Other forms of forest exploitation such as the harvesting of tree backs, gums and rubber were only allowed if they did not result in plant destruction.

Decree no. 46/126 of May 3, 1946 was the third forestry legislation enacted by the French colonial administration in French Cameroon. This Decree classified forest into *Domaine Classé* and *Domaine Protégé*. The former consisted of forest reserves within which users' rights were either prohibited or regulated, while the latter covered unclassified forests. The Decree attributed all forests to the State. Article 2 of this Decree stipulated that *les forêts vacantes et sans maître* (vacant forests without masters) including fallow lands under regeneration were owned by the State. It follows from this provision that local communities were deprived from forest ownership since the only lands which were not vacant were either their farms or plantations.

Though the 1946 Decree was repealed by Ordinance no. 61/14 of November 16, 1961, the new legislation did not solve the forest tenure problems of local communities. It rather entrenched State's control over forest resources including trees planted by individuals.[53]

Upon acceding to independence, the authorities in East Cameroon enacted law no. 68/1/COR of July 18, 1968, regulating forest resources in the French speaking area of the country. This law remained in force until April 1973.

The British regulated non-timber forest products (NTFP) by applying the Nigeria Forestry Ordinance, Chapter 74 of the 1938 Laws

---

[52] Ngwasiri (n 3).
[53] Tumnde (n 4) 358.

of Nigeria.[54] The 1938 Ordinance remained the only piece of legislation governing forest resources in the English speaking parts of Cameroon until April 1973. The Ordinance classified the following as forest products: timber, plants, surface oil, minerals, beeswax and all produce of animal origin found in or brought out from the forest.[55]

Since reunification in 1972 Cameroon has enacted three pieces of legislation dealing with the management of forest resources. The first was Ordinance no. 73/18 of 22 May 1973 and its Decree of application no. 74/357 issued on the 17th of April 1974 almost a year later. This Ordinance which dealt exclusively with forest resources was aimed at "rationalising forestry resources."[56]

This Ordinance recognised the rights of indigenous population to harvest and use secondary forest products such as palm, raphia, bamboos, rattan and edible products. The rights could not, by virtue of section 10 and 25 be exercised without permission, on totally protected areas such as reserves created by the State. Similarly section 20 subjects the harvesting of naturally growing trees to an authorisation granted by the Minister of Agriculture who was in charge of forest at the time.[57]

The second, Law no. 81/13 of 27 November 1981 to lay down Forestry, Wildlife and Fisheries Regulations. This law was accompanied in 1983 by the following Decrees of application:

- Decree no. 83-169 of 12th April 1983 to lay down Forestry Regulations;
- Decree no. 83-170 of 12th April 1983 relating to Wildlife Regulations;
- Decree no. 83-171 of 12th April 1983 to lay down Fisheries Regulations.

The 1981 law repealed the 1973 Ordinance. As stated by Tumnde,[58] there was no substantial change in policy orientation. This law recognised the local communities' users' rights which, like the previous law, were restricted in protected areas. The scope of this law was not limited to forest resources as was the case with the 1973 Ordinance, but was extended to wildlife and fisheries resources.

---

54 Southern Cameroon was administered by Britain as part of its Nigerian protectorate. This conferred on Britain by virtue of article 9 of the 1922 Cameroon Mandatory Agreement powers to introduce Nigerian Laws into Southern Cameroon.

55 Ngwasiri (n 3).

56 "*La rationalisation de nos resources forestières.*" Per Amadou Ahidjo, cf. Tumnde (n4) 358.

57 cf. Funwie (n 9) 13.

58 cf. Tumnde (n 4) 359.

The third, Law no. 94/01 of 20th January 1994 to lay down Forestry, Wildlife and Fisheries Regulations, (hereinafter referred to as the Forestry Law) which devolved powers to local communities to manage forest resources by introducing the concept of community forests, will be given full consideration later. The 1994 law was followed in 1995 by three Decrees of application:

- Decree no. 95/466/PM of 20th July 1995 to lay down the conditions for the implementation of the wildlife regulations, (hereinafter referred to as the Wildlife Decree) which completed the legislation on wildlife by defining certain key terms used in the law such as those clarified in the introductory chapter of this work, and relevant to us because of the role of wildlife in plant propagation.

- Decree no. 95/531/PM of 23rd August 1995 to determine the conditions for the implementation of forestry regulations, (hereinafter referred to as the Forestry Decree). This decree defined key terms completing the legislation on forestry.

- Decree no. 95/413 of 20 June 1995 establishing the modalities for the application of the fishery regulations. This decree which complete the legislation on fishery is not within the scope of this work.

As mentioned earlier, the 1973 Ordinance dealt exclusively with forest resources, whereas the 1981 and 1994 laws were given a wider scope, dealing with forestry wildlife and fisheries resources. The 1994 law currently in force (constitutes our principal piece of legislation in this work), is our focus, because as a consolidating piece of legislation, it has certainly taken into account the loopholes of the previous pieces of legislation.[59] This law is composed of 7 parts and made up of 171 sections. Part 3 addresses forests concerns generally, and sections 37 and 38 specifically deal with community forests, which invariably implements the 1992 Convention on Biological Diversity (CBD) to which Cameroon is a party.

[59] Fonyam, J. B., "The Legal Protection of Forest: A Case Study of Cameroon," in Dunlop, J. and Roy, W. (eds) Culture and Environment. A Reader in Environmental Education, Compiled by Staff from the University of Buea, Cameroon and the Former International Unit, University of Strathcyde, Scotland, U.K (this document has no year of publication and no pagination)

2.3: Legal Framework for the Integration of Indigenous Communities In Natural Resource Management

By legal framework for community forests, we are referring to all forms of laws and regulations that govern community forests initiatives in Cameroon. These range from international agreements to State regulations.

2.3.1: International Involvement Promoting the Participation of Local Communities in Forest Management

Biodiversity conservation and management of natural resources is mostly initiated by bilateral and multilateral agencies which do most of the policies planning.[60] International environmental law and cooperation played a great role in the institution of community forests in Cameroon[61] and Africa as a whole. They are embodied in conventions (treaties) among States and to a greater extent in international declarations invariably defined as "the collective body of agreement among States regarding mutual rights and obligations affecting the environment."[62] Conventions are legally binding and are considered "hard" law.[63] According to article 2 of the 1969 Vienna Convention on the Law of Treaties, they can be called by a variety of names such as treaty, protocol, covenant, pact, act etc. Declarations on the other hand are generally not legally binding and often referred to as "soft" law.

2.3.1.1: "Soft" Law Instruments

International environmental law is based principally on negotiation and political relationships to define the rights and obligations of States. When these negotiations are contained in declarations they constitute "soft" laws having only a persuasive and not a binding force. Though "soft" law is not enforceable, the concept is however relevant in the field of environmental law, because it serves as a prelude or gives direction for the adoption of "hard" instruments law.

---

60 Manga, B. E., "Cameroon's Biodiversity Conservation Policy: The Case of the Mount Cameroon Project" A Doctoral (3ème cycle) Thesis, IRIC, Yaounde, February 2000, p. 61.

61 MINEF, "The Setting Up of Community Forests in Cameroon," Report on the Forum for the Sharing of Field Experience, Nguelemendouka, 14th -17th November 2000, pp. 3 and 7.

62 Percival, R. V et al., Environmental Regulation, Law Science and Policy, IBC, 1999, p. 23.

63 See Chi, A. M., "Understanding International Environmental Declarations: The 2003 AFLEG Declaration and Action Plan," in Juridis Périodique. Revue de Droit et de Science Politique No. 59, 2004, p. 107.

The concept of "soft" law enables States to reach agreements much quicker and has a moral weight for member States of these declarations to implement provisions in their own countries, through legislative processes. Amongst the "soft" law instruments recommending participation of local communities in the management of natural resources are the 1972 Stockholm Declaration on Human Environment, the 1992 Rio Declaration on Environment and Development and the 1999 Yaounde Declaration on the conservation of the Congo Basin Forest.[64]

2.3.1.1.1 The Influence of the 1972 Stockholm Declaration

The involvement of the international community in environmental issues started in 1972, when the United Nations convened the first conference on human environment at Stockholm from the 5th -16th of June 1972. From this conference, emerged the Stockholm Declaration on the Human Environment. The Declaration contains 26 legal principles that have become the foundation for a vast network of international agreements. Two of these principles are relevant to this study. These are Principles 21,[65] which directs that each State has the sovereign right to use its natural resources, but also has the corresponding duty to ensure that its activities do not cause harm outside its boundaries. And principle 4[66] which links environmental protection with human rights and emphasize the duty of each person to safeguard the environment thus requesting the participation of all citizens including local communities in the management of environmental resources of which forest is an indispensable component.

This declaration coincided with the re-unification of Cameroon,[67] and gave rise to the enactment of a national Forestry Ordinance in 1973. This Ordinance which dealt exclusively with forest resource management throughout the national territory supposedly implemented provisions of the above declaration as concerns the sovereign rights over its forest resources.

---

64 CBFP, The Forest of the Congo Basin, State of the Forest 2006, p. 5.

65 "States have, in accordance with the Charter of the United Nations and the principles of international law, the sovereign right to exploit their own resources pursuant to their own environmental policies, and the responsibility to ensure that activities within their jurisdiction or control do not cause damage to the environment of other States or of areas beyond the limits of national jurisdiction."

66 Man has a special responsibility to safeguard and wisely manage the heritage of wildlife and its habitat, which are now gravely imperiled by a combination of adverse factors. Nature conservation, including wildlife, must therefore receive importance in planning for economic development.

67 Cameroon became a Unitary State on the 20th of May 1972. For more on this see Edie, J. T., Civic and Moral Education for Cameroon Schools, CEP, Limbe, 1985, p. 1.

2.3.1.1.2: The 1992 Rio Declaration on Environment and Development

This declaration proclaims principles aimed at promoting the participation of local communities in the management of environmental resources. Principle 10 for instance provides that "environmental issues are best handled with the participation of all concerned citizens…" This provision is buttressed by principle 22 which stresses that indigenous people and their communities, and other local communities, have a vital role in environmental management and development because of their knowledge and traditional practices. States are therefore called upon to recognize and duly support the effective participation of local communities in the sustainable management of environmental resources.

2.3.1.1.3: Agenda 21

Agenda 21 is a global environmental programme and statement of principles emphasizing sustainable development agreed to at the Earth Summit in Rio de Janerio in 1992. Chapter 10 of Agenda 21 calls on governments to make use of traditional and indigenous knowledge and practices in the management of environmental resources. In order to conserve biological diversity, combat deforestation, desertification and drought, chapter 23 and 26 call for the participation of all social groups including local communities and the use of traditional methods of agriculture, agro-forestry, forestry and wildlife management.

2.3.1.1.4: The 1999 Yaounde Declaration

In addition to their commitment at international and continental levels, central African States committed themselves within the sub-region to ensure the rational management of forests and other environmental resources. This sub-regional initiative started in 1992, with the creation of *Programme de la Conservation et d'Utilisation Rationnelle des Ecosystèmes Forestiers en Afrique Centrale* (ECOFAC). This programme which aimed at conserving and sustainably managing forest ecosystem of Central Africa was financed by the European Development Fund (EDF). This was followed in 1995 by a United States Aid for International Development (USAID) planned 20 years initiative known as the Central Africa Regional Programme for the Environment (CARPE), aimed at promoting the sustainable management of forest ecosystem of the

Congo Basin.[68] It equally intends to reduce the rate of deforestation and loss of biodiversity by building the capacity of those involved in forest management both at the local, national and regional levels.

In May 1996, the first conference on the Moist Tropical Forests of Central Africa (*Conférence Sur les Ecosystèmes des forêts Denses et Humides D'Afrique Centrale* (CEFDHAC)) held in Brazzaville for the member States to reflect on the sustainable management of the central African forest. In the course of this conference representative of nine central African States[69] adopted the 1996 Brazzaville Declaration re-iterating their commitment to collaborate in the conservation of the region's forests.

Inspired by the determination reached at the Brazzaville conference, political leaders expressed their desire to collaborate in forest conservation and held a summit in Yaounde in March 1999 to discuss problems related to conservation and the sustainable management of forest resources of the Congo Basin. This summit attended by six Heads of States[70] of Central African countries was aimed at discussing problems related to conservation and the sustainable management of forest resources of the Congo Basin. It led to the signing of the 1999 Yaounde Declaration recognised by the UN 54th General Assembly on 1/2/2000 in a resolution entitled "Conservation and Sustainable Development of Central African Ecosystems.[71] The Heads of States agreed on 12 actions amongst which was to "speed up the process of involvement of rural populations in forest planning and in sustainable management of forest ecosystems."

The "soft" law instruments discussed above directly or indirectly implemented existing "hard" law instruments or paved the way for the adoption of some, such as, the COMIFAC Treaty as elaborated below.

---

[68] For more on this see Chi A. M., "COMIFAC Treaty-First African Regional "Hard" Law on conservation of forest ecosystem in central Africa-A sleeping Treaty? In Juridis Périodique. Revue de Droit et de Science Politique No. 78, 2009, p. 85.

[69] Burundi, Cameroon, Central African Republic, Democratic Republic of Congo, the Republic of Congo (Brazzaville) Equatorial Guinea, Gabon, Rwanda, Sao Tome and Principe.

[70] These were the Heads of States of:
- the Central African Republic;
- the Republic of Burundi;
- the Republic of Cameroon;
- the Republic of Congo;
- the Republic of Equatorial Guinea;
- the Republic of Gabon;

Four other countries acceded to the Declaration and by implication became parties to the Declaration. These were the Democratic Republic of Congo in 2002, and the Republic of Chad, Republic of Rwanda, Republic of Sao Tome and Principe in 2005.

[71] Resolution A/RES/54/214.

2.3.1.2 "Hard" Law Instruments

These are agreements between States considered as having a binding force, variedly referred to as treaties, accords, conventions, agreements, or protocols adopted bilaterally, regionally or multilaterally.[72] Some "hard" law instruments requesting the participation of local communities in the management of forests resources include the 1992 CBD, 1992 Convention on Climate Change, 2003 Maputo Conventions on Nature and Natural Resources and 2005 COMIFAC Treaty.

2.3.1.2.1: The 1992 Convention on Biological Diversity

The process of environmental concern initiated by the 1972 Stockholm conference gave birth to a Declaration, culminating with a 1992 UN Declaration and Convention on the Environment and Development at Rio de Janeiro, Brazil, in an Earth Summit referred to by some authors as *grande messe Mondiale*.[73] This convention articulates principles to promote a new and "equitable global partnership"[74] and stresses the fact that environmental issues are best handled when all citizens are given the opportunity to participate in decision-making processes,[75] thus encouraging the participation of local communities in natural resource management.

Recognising the close and traditional dependence of many indigenous and local communities embodying traditional lifestyles on biological resources,[76] the Convention calls on States not only to recognise and duly support the identity, culture and interest of local communities but also their vital roles in environmental management and development based on traditional knowledge and practices. Article 8 (j) provides that:

> each contracting party shall, as far as possible and as appropriate... *subject to its national legislation*, respect, preserve and maintain knowledge, innovations and practices of indigenous and local

[72] Article 38, paragraph 1 of the Statutes of the I. C. J.
[73] c/f Wafo, S., "Les ONG et le Développement du Droit International de L'Environnement, Analyse des Activités Normatives des ONG Environnemental." A Doctoral (3ème cycle) Thesis, IRIC, 2000, p. 3. Also see Zimmerman, Michael. "Environment," Microsoft® Student Encarta 2009, who refers to it as the largest gathering of world leaders in history.
[74] Percival (21) 1145.
[75] Article 10 (c & d) of the 1992 CBD.
[76] See preamble of the 1992 CBD.

> communities embodying traditional lifestyles relevant for the conservation and sustainable use of biological diversity and promote their wider application with the approval and involvement of the holders of such knowledge, innovations and practices and encourage the equitable sharing of the benefits arising from the utilisation of such knowledge, innovations and practices.

The convention clearly recommends the participation of local communities embodying traditional knowledge in the conservation of biological diversity of which forest is an important element. This interest is restated in articles 10 (c), 17 (2) and 18 (4) of the convention. Article 10 (c) is to the effect that: "each contracting Party shall, as far as possible and as appropriate… protect and encourage customary use of biological resources in accordance with *traditional cultural practices* that are compatible with conservation or sustainable use requirements." Article 17 (2) continues that "… exchange of information shall include exchange of results of technical, scientific and … *indigenous and traditional knowledge…*" while article 18 (4) requires that contracting Parties shall, in accordance with national legislation and policies, encourage and develop methods of cooperation for the development and use of technologies, including *indigenous and traditional technologies*, in pursuance of the objectives of this Convention…"

It could be argued that the adjectives "indigenous and local communities" in article 8 (j), "traditional cultural practices" in article 10 (c), "indigenous and traditional knowledge" in article 17 (2) and "indigenous and traditional technologies" in article 18 (4) above, motivated or underpinned government's decision to create community forest in Cameroon where the indigenous knowledge and practices contemplated was to be applied.

2.3.1.2.2: The 1992 Convention on Climate Change

There is a close relationship between climate change and forest. The Convention on Climate Change calls on States to promote and facilitate public participation in addressing climate change and its effects.[77] Forest guarantees NTFP to local communities. Livelihood depends on the forest

[77] Article 6 (a) (iii) 1992 Convention on Climate Change.

and forest ecosystems serves to mitigate the adverse effect of climate change. The 1994 Forestry Law indirectly implements this Convention as various forestry practices including those of community forest have a significant role in helping to slow down the accumulation of carbon dioxide (co2) in the atmosphere that contributes to climate change.

2.3.1.2.3: The 2003 Maputo Convention

Article xvii of the 2003 Maputo Convention calls on State to take necessary measures to ensure the participation of local communities in the process of planning and management of natural resources upon which such communities depend. This provision is buttressed by the 2007 UN Declaration on the rights of indigenous people which provides that:

> Indigenous people have the rights to manifest, practice, develop and teach their spiritual and religious traditions, customs and ceremonies; the rights to maintain, protect and have access in privacy to their religious and cultural sites…[78]

These culminate with article 5 of the convention concerning indigenous and tribal people in independent countries[79] which provides that the right of people "to the natural resource pertaining to their lands shall be specially safeguarded" including the right "to participate in the use, management and conservation of these resources." It is argued that community forest is embedded in the concept of participatory forest management.

The Maputo Convention placed emphases on achieving an appropriate level of local participation at community level through the creation of incentives pertaining to participation in conservation and sustainable use of natural resources.[80] This provision is in line with principle 22 of the 1992 Rio Declaration on Environment and Development which recognises the vital role of local communities in environmental management. Within Africa, countries of the Central African sub-regions have equally taken some engagements all aimed at enforcing the participation of local communities in the management of the sub-region's rich biodiversity. These engagements are contained in the 2005 COMIFAC Treaty discussed below.

[78] Resolution 61/295, United Nations Declaration on the Rights of Indigenous People, 2007 Article 12.
[79] ILO Convention no. 169.
[80] Article xvii of the 2003 Maputo Convention.

2.3.1.2.5: The 2005 COMIFAC Treaty

The abbreviation COMIFAC needs to be clarified. Originally the abbreviation stood for Council of Ministers in-Charge of Forests (COMIFAC) and now Central Africa Forest Commission (COMIFAC), responsible for decision making, coordination and control of the implementation of policies on the sustainable management of forest ecosystem in Central Africa[81] under whose auspices the 2005 Treaty on the Conservation and Sustainable Management of Forest Ecosystems in Central Africa was signed.

COMIFAC Treaty is an internationally binding instrument signed by the Heads of State and Government of ten Central African countries[82] during their second summit held in February 2005, in Brazzaville (Republic of Congo). This Treaty has a regional status since membership is limited only to Central African States.[83] In order to promote the participation of local communities in the sustainable management of the forests, the Treaty calls on member States to "step up efforts to increase the rapid participation of rural populations in the planning and sustainable management of ecosystems and allot adequate areas for their socio-economic development."[84] The ratification of this treaty obliges its parties to ensure the participation of local communities in the sustainable management of forest in their respective countries. This is demonstrated by the existence of community forests in Cameroon,[85] and Gabon[86] and "*forêts des collectivités locales*[87] in the Republic of Congo.

2.3.2: International Organisations

Closely related to International Conventions are the demands of international donor Organisations such as the I.M.F, the World Bank and NGOs. The first two Organisations are financially oriented while NGOs are duly declared national or foreign Associations authorised in accordance with the laws in force and approved by the administration to participate

[81] See article 10 of 2005 COMIFAC Treaty.

[82] The Central African Republic; Democratic Republic of Congo; Republic of Burundi; Republic of Cameroon; Republic of Chad; Republic of Congo; Republic of Equatorial Guinea; Republic of Gabon; Republic of Rwanda; and the Republic of Sao Tome and Principe.

[83] Article 4 of 2005 COMIFAC Treaty.

[84] Ibid article 1.

[85] Article 37 and 38 of the 1994 Forestry Law.

[86] Article 156, Loi no. 16/01/2001 du 31/11/2001 portant Code *Forestier* en Republic Gabonaise.

[87] Article 11, loi no. 16/2000 du 20/11/2000 portant Code *Forestier*.

in the execution of extremely diverse missions of general interest.[88] They intervene especially in the economic, social, cultural, health, sports, educational, and humanitarian sectors or in matters of environmental and human rights protection.[89] Most of them have a particular valuable role in nature conservation.[90] They are described by World Bank as "private Organisations that pursue activities to relieve suffering, promote the interest of the poor, protect the environment and undertake community development."[91] These Organisations provide financial and material support needed for the conservation of natural resources and encourage the participation of local communities in natural resources management.

The World Bank for instance issued an influential forestry paper in 1978. This paper indicated a major shift in its forestry policy away from industrial forestry to forest protection that meets local needs.[92] As stated by Hazell,[93] one of the World Bank's conditions for involvement in conservation policies was for countries to adopt policies that clearly define the role of local communities and promote their active participation in forest management. The Bank presently lays emphasis on projects that promote forests conservation.[94] Specifically, the Bank exhorted Cameroon during its democratic transition to reform its forestry sector through socio-political and institutional changes.[95] This body was also the prime mover in the creation of MINEF and ONADEF.[96]

Food and Agriculture Organisation (FAO) could be considered as the first Organisation to be inspired by the concept of community

---

[88] Jeanrenaud, J. P., "Non Governmental Organizations-Strategies to Enhance the Conservation Value of Investments in the Forest Sector," in Conservation of West and Central African Rainforest, WBEP, no. 1, 1992, p. 318.

[89] Articles 2 and 3 of the Cameroon Law of December 22, 1999 Governing NGOs.

[90] Sayer, J. A., "Development Assistance Strategies to Conserve Africa's Rainforests," in Conservation of West and Central African Rainforest, WBEP, no. 1, 1992, p. 7.

[91] Wells, M. et al., "People and Parks, Linking Protected Area Management with Local Communities," World Bank, WWF, USAID, January 1999, p. 51.

[92] Tchanou. Z., "Development Communautaire et Forêt Communautaire" in Constraints in the Establishment of Community Forest in Cameroon, Report of the fourth General Assemble meeting of CFN, 6th -9th June 2000, Yaounde, p. 21.

[93] Hazell, P and Magrath, W., "Summary of World Bank Forestry Paper," in Conservation of West and Central African Rainforest, WBEP, No. 1, p. 16.

[94] Sayer, J. A., "Institutional Arrangement for Forests Conservation in Africa," in Conservation of West and Central African Rainforest, WBEP No. 1, 1992, p. 310.

[95] Chimere M. D et Oyono P. R., « Instrumentalités et Déficit des Intineraires de Décentralisation de la Gestion des Ressources Naturelles au Cameroun » in Bulletin Arbres, Forêts et Communautés Rurales. No. 15/16 Spécial Cameroun, Décembre 1998, p. 23.

[96] cf. Manga, B. E., "Cameroon's Biodiversity Conservation Policy: The Case of the Mount Cameroon Project" A Doctoral (3ème cycle) Thesis, IRIC, Yaounde, February, 2000, p. 64.

forestry in 1970. When a serious drought hit the Sahel region only trees survived the drought providing wood and ensuring food security.[97] Inspired by this important role of the forest, the Organisation in 1978[98] launched a programme entitled "Forestry for local community development"[99] that was later transformed to Forest, Trees and People Programme"[100] (FTPP). This was a special programme launched to highlight the importance of forest to human livelihood and help individual countries to either initiate or upgrade field programmes in these areas by incorporating local communities in the sustainable management of forest resources.

International attention came to focus on sustainable management and utilisation in relation to the contribution of forests, not only to global environmental benefits but also to the socio-economic development of the communities settled around them. In response to the widespread institutional recognition that sustainable development must address local people's needs,[101] International Law, for instance, chapter 26 of Agenda 21 and article 8 (j) of 1992 CBD call on States to promote community participation in the management of natural resources of which forest is inclusive. Chapter 26 of Agenda 21 recognises and strengthens the role of indigenous people in the management of their "lands." The term "land" here is understood to include the environment of the area which indigenous people traditionally occupy. The 1994 UN Convention to Combat Desertification[102] (UNCCD) requires States to promote and facilitate the participation of local population particularly women and youths in efforts to combat desertification and mitigate the effect of drought. The 1992 UN Convention on Climate Change[103] (UNCCC) equally calls for public participation in addressing climate change and its effects. The implementation of the above cited international conventions requires the participation of local communities in natural resource management. This is materialised in Cameroon through the concept of community forests.

---

97 Tchanou, Z., "Forestry at the Centre of Community Development," in Community Forestry Network no. 005, May 2001, p. 5.
98 FAO, Community Forestry, Ten Years in Review, CFN 7, Rev 1, FAO Rome, 1992, p. 2.
99 Ibid.
100 CFN, Community Forestry Newsletter, No. 001, Dec 1997, p.11.
101 ODA's Review of Participatory Forest Management, Synthesis of Findings, August 1996, p. 3.
102 Article 5.
103 Article 6 (a) (iii).

2.3.3: State Regulations

State regulations refer to national or municipal laws which promote community forests initiatives in the country. These laws range from the supreme law of the country to Ministerial Decisions. The following are relevant:

2.3.3.1: Law no. 96/06 of 18 January 1996 amending the 1972 Constitution

The need to protect our environment and rights to a healthy environment is contained in the preamble of the 1996 Constitution which states that, "every person shall have a right to a healthy environment..." For the above mentioned rights to be assured, the preamble requires that both the government and citizens should in a participatory manner protect the environment. This participatory approach in the management of the environment could be deduced from the following statement: "...the protection of the environment shall be the duty of every citizen. The State shall assure the protection and the improvement of the environment." Considering that the environment consists of natural resources such as forests, participation of local communities for its sustainable management is implied.

With the revision of the 1972 Constitution in 1996, the heated debate on the legal value of the preamble of the Constitution has been laid to rest by the 1996 Constitution in the following words: "the preamble shall be part and parcel of this constitution."[104] In view of this provision, all the provisions in the preamble of the Cameroon Constitution have the force of law and consequently should be implemented. Even though the 1994 Forestry Law that gave birth to the concept of community forests in Cameroon preceded the 1996 Constitution, the latter has a wider scope in that it calls for participation in the management of environmental resources (water, wildlife, land etc) whereas the former was only limited to forests, hence the concept of community forests.

2.3.3.2: Law no. 94/01 of 20th January 1994 to lay down Forestry, Wildlife and Fisheries Regulations

This is the third piece of legislation dealing with forestry issues enacted by the Cameroonian legislature since independence. This law provides for community forests defined as:

---

[104] See Article 65 of the 1996 Cameroon Constitution.

> A forest of the non-permanent State forest, object of a management agreement between a village community and the services in charged of forestry. The management of such a forest shall be the responsibility of the village community concerned with the technical assistance of the service in charge of forestry.[105]

One of the main objectives of this study was to investigate some of the shortcomings of this law and its compatibility with other international instruments in the sustainable management of forests in the country. Because this law subjects the ownership of forests to 1974 land tenure regulations, it deprives local communities of land ownership and by extension forest tenure. Consequently the law equally does not provide for the promotion of indigenous knowledge and customary practices indispensable in participatory forests management. The non-recognition of indigenous tenure constitutes a major drawback in the realisation of indigenous forests as will be discussed in chapter seven.

2.3.3.3: The 1995 Decrees of Application

In order to ease the application or enforcement of the 1994 Forestry Law, three specific regulatory instruments were signed in 1995. The first relates to the implementation of the Forestry Regulations[106] the second on the implementation of Wildlife Regulation[107] and the third on the implementation of fishery regulations.[108] Only the first two are within the scope of this work. The 1995 Forestry Decree completed the legislation on forestry by providing certain requirements for the creation of community forests, which relevance is discussed in chapter four.

2.3.3.4: Law no. 96/12 of 5th August 1996 relating to Environmental Management

The 1996 Environmental Law which came into force some eight months after the 1996 Constitution directly implemented the Constitution.

105 Article 3 (11) of the 1995 Forestry Decree.

106 Decree no. 95/531/PM of 23rd August to determine the conditions for the implementation of the forestry regulations.

107 Decree no. 95-466-PM of 20 July 1995 to lay down the conditions for the implementation of wildlife regulations.

108 Decree no. 95/413 of 20 June 1995 to determine certain modalities for the application of the fishery regulations.

This is based on the fact that the law just like the Constitution which preceded it calls on the participation of local communities in environmental management as is evident in the following provision:

> ...the President of the Republic shall define the national environmental policy. Its implementation shall devolve upon the government which shall apply it in collaboration with the decentralised territorial authorities, grassroots communities and environmental protection Associations.[109]

The role of grassroots or local communities in the management of the environment is demonstrated as law gives competence to traditional authorities to use customary norms to settle disputes relating to the use of some natural resources, such as water.[110] By traditional authorities in this context we are referring to Chiefs and Fons who incarnate customary, administrative and judicial powers at the local level. They are organised and classified into categories by Ordinance no. 77/245 of 15 July 1977 on the organisation of Chieftaincies,[111] surprisingly they are not formally recognized nor have legal status as far as the management of indegenous forest is concerned as explored in chapter five.

2.3.3.5: The 1998 Manual of the Procedure for the Attribution and Norms for the Management of Community Forests

This Manual legally approved in April 1998 by the Ministry of Environment and Forestry[112] was sponsored by bilatcral donors, precisely the British Council and the Canadian Fund for Support of Grassroots Initiatives. This Manual recaps the legal and regulatory framework for the creation and management of community forests. It guides the community in the preparation of the application file, SMP, Management agreement etc. It equally enhances the process involved in the acquisition and management of community forests by providing the legal procedure in channeling community forests management agreements from the local community through the local forestry officials to MINFOF. The Manual also provides some annexes ranging from the models of community

---

[109] Article 3 of the 1996 Environmental Law.

[110] Ibid article 93 (1).

[111] Article 2 of this Ordinance classified traditional rulers into first, second and third degree chiefs.

[112] Décision No. 253/D/MINEF/DF. Portant Adoption du Document Intitulé « Manuel de Procédure d'Attribution et des Normes de Gestion des Forets Communautaires ».

forests management agreements to minutes of consultative meetings, all aimed at assisting local communities in the preparation, submission and implementation of their management plans and agreements. This Manual was reviewed in 2009 to simplify the procedure of acquiring and managing community forests. The procedural modification introduced by this new manual will be discussed in chapter eight.

How versed are the local people with this Manual is doubtful, given that most of the community forests in our study sites were either created by Pilot projects, NGOs or local elites, some for their selfish interests.[113] The case of COFAYET Bengbis Community forest is a good example as it does not meet the aspirations of the local community in terms of provision of socio-economic amenities for sustainable livelihood.

2.3.4: Customary Law

Many definitions have been proffered for customary law. Section 2 of the Evidence Ordinance Cap 62, of the revised Laws of the Federation of Nigeria 1958 defines customary as "... a rule which in a particular district has from long usage obtained the force of law." Section 18 (1) (a) of the Customary Court Ordinance, Cap 142 of the revised Laws of the Federation of Nigeria 1958 also describes customary law as:

> "the native law and customs prevailing in the jurisdiction of the court so far as it is not repugnant to natural justice, equity and good conscience, nor incompatible with any written law for the time being in force."[114]

Customary law is equally referred to by some authors "as the generally accepted usage in any given group"[115] and as "the body of law deriving from established local customs and usages of a tribe or community."[116] It is equally referred to as "native laws and customs, traditional laws or autochthonous laws"[117] and varies according to various communities.

---

[113] Fonkem, S. N., "Rape of the Forest: Sacrificing Trees for Wood," in Insight Magazine, no. 003, May 2003, p. 21.

[114] See also *Ngeh V. Ngome* (1962-64) WCLR 321, *Immaculate Wanga Vefonge V. Samuel Lyonga Yukpe* (1981) CASWP/CC/25/81 (unreported).

[115] Ngwafor, E. N., Family law in Anglophone Cameroon, University of Regina Press, Saskatchewan, Canada, 1993, p. 8.

[116] Anyangwe, C., The Cameroon Judicial System, Ceper, Yaounde, 1987, p. 239.

[117] Ibid.

All above cited definitions stress the fact that customary law is the sum total of rules of conduct established by long usage and tradition and obligatory on those within its scope. Another definition is that advanced by Obi,[118] as "... a rule (or body of rules) which the members of a given community recognise as binding on themselves and which the court will enforce if and when called to do so."

The application of these rules in Anglophone Cameroon is guaranteed by section 27 (1) of the SCHCL 1955 which directs the High Court to observe and enforce the observance of any customary law rule which is not repugnant to natural justice, equity and good conscience nor incompatible either directly or by natural implication with any written law for the time being in force.[119] It is also, a well-established principle of law in francophone Cameroon that a rule of customary law is to be excluded if it is contrary to the notion of *bonnes mœurs* et *ordre public.*[120] This implies that custom will not be enforced if it is repugnant to natural justice, equity and good conscience or if it is incompatible with any written law for the time being in force as was the case in *Ngeh V. Ngome*[121] and *Immaculate Wanga Vefonge V. Samuel Lyonga Yukpe.*[122]

In practical terms, management of forests using indigenous institutions is manifested in the conservation of sacred forests where according to Dr. Chi[123] beliefs and myths function as *de facto* forest conservation assets or incentives. Because customary laws are generally embedded in local institutions, the creation of new institutions to replace existing ones for the management of community forests compromises the regulation of community forest to be explored in chapter five.

2.4: Integrated Natural Resource Management Institutions

The Institutions that promote and regulate community forest initiatives in Cameroon may be grouped into two. These are: modern or

---

[118] Obi, C., Modern Family Law in Southern Nigeria, London, Sweet & Maxwell, 1966, p. 70.

[119] *Ngeh V. Ngome* (1962-64) WCLR 321, *Immaculate Wanga Vefonge V. Samuel Lyonga Yukpe* (1981) CASWP/CC/25/81 (unreported).

[120] cf. Ewang, A. S., "The Place of Customary Law in the Cameroonian Legal System," in Fundamina, UNISA, 2001, p. 71.

[121] (1962-64) WCLR 321.

[122] (1981) CASWP/CC/25/81 (unreported).

[123] Chi, A. M., "Legal recognition of sacred forests in Cameroon: Giving customary communal ownership rights statutory tenure rights," in Bojang, F. et al (eds.) Natural Resource Tenure Systems and their Implication for Agriculture, Food security and Nature conservation in Africa, Nature and Faune, vol. 24. Issue 2, FAO, Accra, Ghana, 2010, p. 26.

State institutions on the one hand, and local or traditional institutions on the other.

2.4.1: State Institutions

This refers to the Ministries of Forestry and Wildlife (MINFOF), Environment and Nature protection and sustainable development (MINEPDED), and other related Institutions.

2.4.1.1: Ministry of Forestry and Wildlife

Before 2004, it was MINEF[124] created in 1992 which was the principal government structure or institution offering opportunity for community forests in Cameroon. With Presidential Decree no. 2004/320 of 8 December 2004, this Ministry was divided into two, MINFOF and MINEP with distinct functions[125] which are nevertheless interrelated for various reasons such as in the domain of climate change. For instance uncontrolled deforestation will have a negative effect on climate change while reforestation will have a positive effect on climate change. Since forest management falls within the scope of MINFOF while climate change adaptation measures are managed by MINEP, these two ministerial Departments must therefore work in synergy.

MINFOF has been decentralised at the Regional, Divisional and Sub-Divisional levels[126] to solve the forestry and wildlife problems of local communities. In order to appreciate the institutional framework offered by this Ministry for forest management, it will be relevant for us to study its structural organisation.

Decree no. 2005/099 of 6th April 2005[127] placed this Ministry under the authority of a Minister, charged with the elaboration, implementation and evaluation of government policy in matters of forestry and wildlife, such as the management and protection of the national forest estate from which community forests are created. To attain government objectives in participatory forestry hence the creation of community forests, a Sub- Directorate of community forest

---

124 This Ministry was created in 1992, by Decree no. 92/069 of 9th April 1992 modifying the administrative Structure of Cameroon.

125 Articles 5 (19) and 5 (21) of Decree no. 2004/320 of 8 December 2004.

126 Article 70 of Decree no. 2005/099 of 6th April Relating to the Organisation of the Ministry of Forestry and Wildlife.

127 Ibid article 1 (1).

was created, with three services placed under its control headed by Chiefs of services. These services are:

- The Service in charge of reservations and SMP: This service ensures the reservation of community forests as well as receives studies and approves SMP,[128] supposedly the relevant service to guide communities in the conception and establishment of community forest programmes.

- The Service charged with the follow up of community forests activities and litigations: This Service receives and studies various applications for the exploitation of community forests and also follows up litigations related to community forests,[129] supposedly responsible for enforcing sanctions on illegal activities perpetuated in community forests.

- The Information, Sensitisation and Formation Service: This service coordinates and supervises sensitisation and training programmes related to community forests. It is also charged with the elaboration, up-date and vulgarisation of the Manual of Procedure and Norms for the Management of Community Forests.[130] This service certainly contributed to the recent revision of the manual of procedure and norms for the management of community forests.

The decentralised services of MINFOF are composed of the Regional and Divisional Delegations and Forestry Posts. Matters dealing with community forests at the Regional level are treated by the Regional Chief of Service for Forestry[131] under the authority of the Regional Delegate. He is equally charged with classified forests in the Region such as State and council forests.

Working in close collaboration with the Regional Delegates are Divisional Delegates who head the Divisional Delegations. They are charged with the coordination, elaboration, animation and control of the activities of MINFOF within the Division.[132] Within the Divisional Delegations are Sections or Forests Services. Though the organigramme

---

128 Ibid article 37.
129 Ibid article 38.
130 Ibid article 39.
131 Ibid article 73.
132 Ibid article 77.

does not specify the duties of these services, we discovered in the course of field work that they handle matters pertaining to community forests at the Divisional Level. An example is that, we realised for instance that there is a community forests unit in some Delegations, such as that in the Delegation of MINFOF for the Haut Nyong at Abong Mbang in the East Region, known as "cellule de forêt communautaire".

There are also Forestry Posts created by the Minister when need arises[133] to control forestry and wildlife activities, as well as illegal exploitation of community forests within their areas of competence.[134] Most of these Posts exist at the level of Sub-Divisions and hardly have information to offer as far as community forests management activities are concerned.[135] These Posts most often have only one personnel and a poor filing system.

2.4.1.2: Ministry of Environment Nature Protection and Sustainable Development (MINEPDED)

This Ministerial Department has among other duties to define rational measures for the management of natural resources in collaboration with other Ministries concerned. It has to inform and encourage public participation in the management and protection of the environment.[136] Unfortunately, MINEP is not involved with the creation and management of community forests since this falls within the attributions of MINFOF. The duties of MINEP therefore seem not to be complementary with those of MINFOF. For instance, we observed that on the national tree planting day in Buea in 2010, the personnel of the MINEP were not concerned with the planting of trees within the Buea municipality. This was exclusively done by MINFOF whereas MINEP ought to have carried out environmental impact assessment before exotic species or trees are planted. It is commendable that MINEP be involved to ensure that EIA are carried out before the exploitation of community forests such as sale of standing volume because community forest provides ecosystem services like any other forests.

---

[133] Ibid Article 78 (1).

[134] Ibid article 78 (2).

[135] In Santa Sub-division for instance where there are two community forests under creation, the Chief of Forestry Post had no information related to these forests.

[136] Article 1(2) of Decree no. 2005/117 relating to the Organisation of the Ministry of Environment and Nature Protection.

2.4.1.3: Other Related Ministries

Other Ministerial Departments having an influence in the management of forests in general according to Ngbwa[137] include the Ministry of Agriculture and Rural Development (MINADER) charged with elaborating and executing government policy in the agricultural sector. Though not directly implicated in the management of community forest, MINADER has an unbreakable relation with the forestry sector since forest and agriculture generally share the same parcel of land in rural areas. Where concern is given to agriculture, the likelihood is that forest will be destroyed as was the case within the Laikom Community Forest found in the North West Region. To overcome deforestation in community forests, agro-forestry should be encouraged and this included in community forests management plans. The Information, Sensitisation and Formation Service of the Sub-Directorate of community forest could work in synergy with MINADER and sensitise local communities on agro-forestry.

The Ministry of Scientific Research and Innovation (MINRESI) responsible for the national herbarium also has authority to collect and use forest genetic resources for scientific purposes. Placed under the authority of this Ministry are some biodiversity related public Institutes such as the Institution of Agronomic Research and Development (IRAD) and the Institution of Medical Research and Medicinal Plants Studies (IMPM). The former carries out research required for agriculture, wildlife conservation and forest regeneration while the latter makes use of the existing wealth of medicinal plants to produce effective medicines. The indiscriminate exploitation of these plants has a negative effect on protected species and may lead to the extinction of endemic species. For instance the high demand for *prunus Africana* has resulted in over exploitation of this plant in community forests in Boyo Division, in the North West Region. However the herbarium offers opportunities for research for new plants that can be introduced in community forests.

No project can effectively be implemented without finances. The Ministry of Finance therefore has an important role as far as the creation and management of community forests are concerned. It is the duty of

---

137 For more on the role of various Ministries in forest management, see Ngbwa, A. F., "La Banque mondiale et le Secteur Forestier au Cameroun" Mémoire présenté et soutenu publiquement en vue de L'obtention du Diplôme D'Etudes Supérieures Spécialisées (DESS), IRIC, Yaounde, 2002.

this Ministry to determine the value and recover various taxes derived from forest exploitation based on Finance Law. It is also the duty of this Ministry to provide the budget needed by MINFOF to execute its activities. It is recommended that taxes from community forests exploitation be redeployed for the management of these forests.

The Ministry of Higher Education (MINESUP) equally intervenes in community forests through programmes aimed at training foresters. The Faculty of Agronomy and Agricultural Science (FASA) of the University of Dschang runs a Department for the training of foresters. Forestry courses are equally offered by the Forestry school of Mbalmayo and the Wildlife school of Garoua. It is expected that the curriculum takes into consideration local reality, especially indigenous knowledge indispensable in the management of community forests. This means a combining scientific and traditional knowledge is needed for the management of community forests.

2.4.2: Local Community Legal Entities

In order to qualify to sign community forests management agreements with government, the local community must have a legal personality in the form of an entity in keeping with the law.[138] This could either be an Association, Common Initiative Group, (CIG) Economic Interest Group (EIG) or a Cooperative Society. These legal entities are not only largely different but completely inadaptable to local realities. Unfortunately they are not only new to local people but are governed by rules and motives not intended for the conservation of natural resources, let alone the management of community forest. Given that these legal entities replaced existing indigenous legal institutions such as "chiefs" sanctioned by another law[139] is a contradiction as elucidated below.

2.4.3: Existing Traditional Institutions

Talking of local or traditional institutions, we are referring to indigenous organisations existing at village levels. In Cameroon, which is a racial cross-road, a hotchpotch of several dozen petty tribes,[140] there

138 Section 28 (3) of the 1995 Forestry Decree.

139 See article 1 and 2 of Decree No. 77/245 of July 1977 on the Organisation of Chieftaincy.

140 Anyangwe, C., "Land Tenure and Interests in Land," in Cameroon Law Review, 2rd series Nr 27, 1984, p. 31.

exist about 250[141] tribes or villages with defined institutions. Each of these villages has and enforces customary laws which are legally recognised in the country.[142] Some of these customs have evolved over the centuries, as different ethnic groups developed their own concept of sustainable management of natural resources in a way which has enabled them to live in harmony with their environment. In some communities, traditional law and customary practices even offer reliable, cheaper and effective methods of environmental protection.[143] The exploitation of existing local institutions such as the Chiefs, Fons, Lamidos, in our view will enhance participation envisaged by the law, than legal entities such as "cooperatives" that are economic or profit driven.

Considering that the South-East parts of the country is composed of acephalous communities, where traditional institutions and practices for forest management are not well developed,[144] our study of traditional institutions will therefore be limited to the western grass field, precisely the North-West Region which has similar traditions with the West Region of the country. In the North-West Region, the traditional institutions for the management of forest and its resources are well structured under the customary administration of each village headed by a Chief or Fon. In Kom and Oku for instance where the bulk of community forests within the Region are situated, the village structures responsible for the management of the forest before the advent of community forest include the Kwihfon, the Fon, the Traditional Council, the Village Council and the quarter heads. These are organs within a chieftaincy which is a legal entity recognised by law with competences relevant to the sustainable management of community forests.

2.4.3.1: The Kwihfon

This is a traditional society composed of men with supreme powers. It is the highest traditional organ in Oku[145] while in Kom,[146] it occupies the second

---

141 See also Gaillard, P., Le Cameroun Tome 1, Editions L'Harmttan, Paris, 1989, p.13, where he rather talks of 207 tribes and consequently 207 customs.

142 See section 27 of S.C.H.C.L 1955.

143 Manga, C. F., "The Effectiveness of Environmental Protection Measures in Cameroon's 1994 Law laying Down Forestry, Wildlife and Fisheries Regulations," in Journal of Environmental Law Vol. 9, no. 1, Oxford University Press (OUP)1997, p. 47.

144 Cf. Ngwasiri, C. N., "The Community Forestry Programme in Cameroon: A Participatory Management Option?" CIFOR, working paper No. 5, December 2000, p. 32.

145 Oku is a patrilineal society where kwihfon is considered the most important in the hierarchy of traditional institutions.

146 Kom is a matrilineal society where kwihfon occupies the second position in the hierarchy of traditional institutions.

place in the hierarchy of traditional and indigenous organs of a chieftaincy. Be it the first or second organ, the Kwihfon has similar or same functions within a chieftaincy as far as its role in forest management is concerned.

In communities where the Kwihfon is considered the most important organ, it is the owner of all lands within the said village including forestland and this even includes the people.[147] In communities where the Fon or Chief is considered the owner of the land, the technical aspect of management and protection of the said land is the responsibility of the Kwihfon. Thus, whether the first or second important organ in the village, technically it is the responsibility of Kwihfon to manage and protect community land, endowed with traditional norms, the use of natural resources such as forests that underpins rural livelihoods. For instance in Bambui village, Kwihfon is said to have secretly instructed all men to possess dane guns in preparation for a war against Funge people considered to illegally claim ownership of portions of Bambui land.[148]

The attribution of the village land to the Fon or Kwihfon is theoretical as this will be contrary to the existing land legislation within the country. Practically ownership of land in the country is by land title acquired under conditions provided by the land legislation. The applicant must be a Cameroonian and show proof of occupation and exploitation before 5th August 1974.[149] In no community has the Fon got the land title of the entire village. On the other hand, it is inconceivable that Kwihfon which no one has ever seen could have a land title. Paradoxically the recognition of this organ as the owner and manager of all village land is acknowledged and respected by individuals with land titles. To the extent that, within village communities, a corpse cannot be buried even on titled land without Kwihfon's permission, for this will amount to trespass onto Kwihfon's land. In the circumstance, the question is who then is the de jure owner of land in general and community forest land in particular?

Kwihfon which no one has ever seen lives in perpetuity, enacts and enforces laws as is the case in Oku or simply enforces customary laws

147 In our interview with Shuyfaai Tawoh of Mbah, (2009), we gather that the entire village as a hold belongs to the kwihfon.

148 Nkwi, W. G., "Boundary conflicts in Africa: A case study of Bambili and Babanki-Tungoh (Northwest Province of Cameroon), (1950-1995)," in Journal of applied social sciences, Vol. 6, no. 1&2, University of Buea, Cameroon, 2007, p. 15.

149 Section 9, Decree no. 76-165 of 27 April 1976 to establish the conditions for obtaining land certificates amended and supplemented by Decree no. 2005-481 of 16 December 2005.

enacted by the Fon as it obtains in Kom. Whether enacted by the Fon or Kwihfon, these laws most often take the form of prohibitory injunctions. For instance the people of Kom and Oku were prohibited to farm, graze animal, fell certain species of trees, harvest *prunus Africana*, hunt certain species of birds and animals within the community forests by kwihfon. To regulate illegal exploitation of wildlife in some communities, kwihfon appoints specific hunters, while in other communities hunting seasons and days are organised, to enable the people meet their needs in terms of protein. The Fon just like Kwihfon sanctions defaulters by ordering payment of fines or excommunication.

2.4.3.2: The Fondoms and Chieftaincies

Fons and Chiefs are recognised based on territory and classified under the 1977 Chieftaincy Decree.[150] It is envisaged that on the territory on which they exercise their functions as auxiliaries of the administration,[151] there are natural resources besides forests. Because of their technical nature some organs of the Fondom are charged with the management of these resources.

2.4.3.3: The Traditional Council

It is the technical organ charged with the role of forest in spiritual and religious matters. This Council is made up of representative of all villages of the Fondom. It judges and punishes violation of traditional rules and practices that govern the use of forest such as arson and illegal exploitation of totem plants and animals. For instance, exploitation from shrines and forests within the Bakwere community without the permission of traditional authorities is believed to attract sanction inflicted by spirits.

Within some communities, the totemic relationship is widespread. It is especially strong among some Native Americans and Aboriginal Australians. In these societies, the totem is often regarded as a companion and helper with supernatural powers and as such is respected and occasionally venerated. With the exception of some totemic rituals, killing, eating, or touching the totem is prohibited. Individuals cultivated personal friendship with particular totemic animal or plant,[152] a practice which by and large protects the forest since these totems are generally believed to dwell in the forest.

---

150 Articles 1 and 2 Decree No. 77/245 of July 1977 on the Organisation of Chieftaicy.

151 Ibid article 20.

152 Saliba, John A. "Totemism." Microsoft® Studen Corporation, Encarta 2009.

Aboriginal Australians equally protect sacred sites generally found in the forest. These sites are believed to be the dwelling of *Wondjina*, (ancestral spirits) which travel across Australia establishing the essential fabric of life and depositing the spirits of unborn children.[153] It could be deduced that native Australians believe that forest destruction could be sanctioned by a decrease in birth rate: hence the need to protect the forest.

Because of their usefulness, beauty or fear-inspiring aspects, the *soma* plants and *coca* trees have been worshiped by local communities in India and Peru respectively as totems. These plants are considered either as holy in themselves or as dwelling places for spirits or for the intoxicating property of product derived from them.[154] Plants regarded as harbouring spirits of fertility have equally been worshiped by primitive tribes in Europe.[155] The non-respect of these customary practices is sanctioned by local institutions such as the traditional council.

2.4.3.4: Quarter Heads

Villages are broken down into quarters placed under the authority of quarter heads. Though constituting the last unit in the hierarchy of traditional Institutions, they represent the Fondom at the lowest level. This organ has power at first instance to identify illegal activities related to land matters, the destruction of crops by stray animals etc. As concerns forest management, this organ assists in the suppression of forest crimes by bringing defaulters before superior organs of the Fondom.

2.4.4: Non Recognition of Existing Indigenous Institutions

As stated earlier, article 2 of Decree No. 77/245 of 15 July 1977 classified traditional leaders into three categories made up of first, second and third class chiefs. These chiefs use customary laws to govern their villagers and are given the authority to solve conflicts related to the use and management of natural resources and assist in the prosecution of crimes,[156] for customary justice systems are considered as the cornerstone of disputes resolution within local communities with 80% of disputes being resolved

---

[153] Redmond, W. A., "The Dreaming." Microsoft® Student Corporation, Encarta 2009.
[154] Redmond, W.A., "Nature Worship." Microsoft® Student Corporation, Encarta 2009.
[155] Ibid.
[156] Section 93 (1) 1996 Environmental Law.

through such fora.[157] But when it comes to the management of community forests, none of these institutions is recognised by law. Strangely the 1994 Forestry Law rather refers to civil society organisations such as Association, CIG, Cooperative Societies and EIG which are not representative of local communities. Some are headed by individuals who are resident out of the locality. For instance, the forest management officer (FMO) of Tinto clan community forest is resident in Limbe while that of DIPAN DI LONG is resident in Douala and are not recognised or accountable to the local community as such.

Government seems to have realised the shortcomings of these new institutions and in some cases prefer to collaborate with existing traditional Institutions such as Fons and Chiefs. Conversely, traditional authorities do not recognise these new institutions and have preferred to work directly with government. This was noticed in Belo where having arrested an intruder in the community forest, the administration charged with the supervision of that forest took the culprit rather to the Fon. Similarly the latter request government assistance without consulting the supposed new legal entity. For instance the traditional rulers of Yétyang Ndoundou, Olembé and Meka'a Yétyang wrote to the administration requesting that the management agreement for COFAYET community forest should be cancelled.[158] There is need to reconcile what the law provides and what obtains on the ground for the purpose of legal reforms.

In a broader context, environmental concern caught international attention since the 1972 Stockholm Conference on the Human Environment. In 1992 a CBD called on member States to incorporate local communities in the management of environmental resources. In countries of the Congo Basin, respective governments in an attempt to implement the provision of article 8 (j) of the 1992 CBD have enacted new laws or amended existing ones providing for local population in the management of natural resources.

157 Naomi, J., "Bush Justice in Bougainville: Mediating Change by Changing the Custodianship of Custom, in Harper, E., (ed.) Working with Customary justice Systems: Post-Conflicts and Fragile States, IDLO, 2011, p. 16.

158 See Letter written to the Minister of Environment and Forest through the S.D.O for Dja et Lobo on 21st of December 1997 by the local communities of Yétyang Ndoundou, Olembé and Meka'a Yétyang requesting the cancellation of Arrête No. 0001/A/MINEF/DF/SDIF/SA of the 1st of July 1997 creating the COFAYET BENGBIS community forest. This letter was signed by 19 persons among whom were:

- Ateba Thomas, Chief of Ndoundou village;
- Mendoua Meyanga Moise, Chief of Olembé;
- Moneboulou Edjimbi, chief of Meka'a Yetyang.

The participation of local communities in the management of Cameroon's forestry resources is guaranteed by the 1994 Forestry Law[159] which opened the way for the creation of 'community forests' in the country. This law equally gives local councils the possibility of including forests among their private assets[160] as well as the rights of private individuals to own and manage forests on land belonging to them[161] all aimed at sharing forest management.

In the Republic of Congo, article 36 and 37 of the 2002 Forestry Code offers the possibility for forest in the public domain to be devolved and managed by individuals or local communities.

In Gabon, the classification of forest is completely different from what obtains in Cameroon. Law no. 6/01 of 31/12/01 on the Forestry Code of Gabon stipulates that "any forest forms part of the national domain and is the exclusive property of the Sate."[162] Nevertheless, articles 22 of the Forestry Code of Gabon gives the opportunity for communities to benefit from forests concessions on forestland held by virtue of customary law. In this country, pilot projects are set up and managed as community forests.[163]

In the Democratic Republic of Congo (DRC) the forest is distinguished into classified and protected forest. The former is reserved for conservation while logging may be carried out in the latter. Based on the land tenure which is derived from land concessions, the forestry law has also adopted forest concessions as an exclusive means of access to forest resources. Thus a concession could be granted for the creation of community forests permitting local communities to participate in the management of forest resources. Whereas law no. 011/2002 (Chapter 3) on the Forestry Code of the DRC directly opens the way for the incorporation of local population in forest management by creating community forests.

A reading of Article 53 of the Forestry Code of Central African Republic (CAR) makes it clear that a territorial community may own a forest if such a forest is classified by decree on behalf of the community or if the area was re-forested and managed by the said community.[164]

159 Article 37 of the 1994 Forestry Law.

160 Ibid article 30.

161 Ibid article 29.

162 Loi no.6/01 du 31/12/01 portant Code Forestier.

163 CBFP, The Forest of the Congo Basin, State of the Forest 2006, p. 68.

164 Ibid p. 65.

In other parts of the world participatory forest management is fairly demonstrated in the form of joint forest management (JFM) such as in India collaborative forest management in England and co-management of communal reserves in Peru.[165]

Joint forest management concentrates on degraded forests with main focus on forest regeneration. This system was introduced in India some 30 years ago, with the initial test model developed in West Bengal in the early 1970. The system was facilitated by popular movements claiming rights to forest and the fact that the degradation of forest under state management was increasing. Through JFM local communities commit themselves to protect and manage forest with government. Ownership of the forest remains with State while the communities in association with the State manage the forest resources and share the cost equally. Though offering opportunities for communities to benefit from forest management, many indigenous communities in India considered JFM as very unsatisfactory.[166] Local communities do not play equal role in decision making and the State frequently benefits from community efforts[167] by having a considerable share of benefits derived from exploitation of NTFP. This injustice led to the enactment of the Forest Rights Act in 2006, recognising the land and user rights of communities living in forest areas.[168]

Unlike in Cameroon where community forests are found in rural areas on land owned by the State, in England community forests are based in urban and peri-urban areas on land owned by the State, private individuals and community associations. They developed from government initiative to regenerate cities affected by a decline in industry and rising unemployment.[169] Community forests in England are managed by boards composed of community activists, business representatives, local authority staff and elected members and forestry professionals. This English model is advantageous in that the problem of resource ownership does not exist. Some authors confirm that community forests in England have positive effect on both the environment and the community in the

---

[165] Long, C., Forest and Community control: Official process that permits formal recognition of community management and rights and their relevance to the Democratic Republic of Congo, IIED, 2010, p. 116.

[166] Springate-Baginski et al., The India forest rights Act of 2006: Commoning Enclosures? Available at: http//iasc2008.glos.ac.uk/conference%20papers/papers/S/springate-Bagnski6_233001.pdf (Accessed on 05/06/2011).

[167] Long, (n130) 17.

[168] Ibid p. 18.

[169] Ibid p. 17.

sense that better investment climate have been created in areas where these forests are operational.[170]

In Peru communal reserves, a type of protected area for biodiversity and water catchment is subjected to co-management between communities and the State. These reserves are found on land to which local communities lay traditional claims but are not used on daily basis.[171] The management of communal reserves is unique in the sense that it is supposed to be carried out by Contract Administrator Executor. This is a body composed of representatives of all the communities bordering the reserve and the State department in charge of protected areas. Unless the above mention body is constituted and a management plan agreed neither the State nor the local community has the right to manage or benefit from communal reserves, with the exception of mineral reserved to the State.[172]

2.5: Conclusion

Government has developed legal and institutional frameworks for forest resource management aimed at implementing the 1992 CBD. The legal framework is well established through various pieces of legislations, enacted either by the local legislator or International community. Though these laws provide for the participation of local communities in the management of natural resources, their implementation do not relate to local realities and institutions such as indigenous customs on which local communities are regulated and which they have used from time immemorial to manage their environment.

The 1992 CBD for instance recommends the use of cultural practices and indigenous knowledge in the management of environmental resources. In implementing this convention, the 1994 Forestry Law introduced the concept of community forests to be managed by local communities. This law request for the creation of legal entities which are supposed to manage the forest in sustainable manner. But unfortunately, they are not recognised by local communities and do not make use of cultural practices and indigenous knowledge in the management of community forests.

170 See http//www.commuityforest.org.uk/resources/evaluation_report.pdf (Last consulted 10/06/2011).

171 Long, (n 130) 16.

172 Ibid.

Local indigenous institutions have been replaced by legal modern entities in the management of community forest. Local communities do not collaborate with these new entities because their cultural practices do not conform to them. Thus in as much as the Forestry Law attempts to implement the 1992 CBD it fails to make use of local institutions endowed with practices and indigenous knowledge which is the principal requirement of article 8 (j) of the 1992 CBD. The replacement of indigenous institutions with legal entities that do not represent local communities presupposes the distortion of the concept of community forest where the principal stakeholders are the local communities as discussed in chapter five.

So long as these laws have identified and recognised modern institutions or stakeholders, (Association, CIG, EIG, Cooperative societies) rather than indigenous institutions which represent local communities, the concept of community forest will remain misapprehended. The 1992 CBD clearly states that a local community is characterised by indigenous knowledge and traditional practices which modern institutions lack.

A review of laws of some countries in the Congo Basin has revealed a gloomy situation. The call for participatory forestry in the 1992 CBD has not been implemented by the adoption of national laws that gives a picture of government working with the true representative of local communities. This is crucial because local communities endowed with indigenous knowledge have big contribution to make in the sustainable management of forest. This has been proven in some countries such as India, Peru, and Nepal where the management and ownership of forest has been devolved to local communities.

CHAPTER THREE

BENEFITS DERIVED FROM INTEGRATING INDIGENOUS COMMUNITIES IN THE MANAGEMENT OF ENVIRONMENTAL RESOURCES

3.1: Introduction

Forests represent a major natural resource and occupy an intermediate position in the spectrum of natural resources.[173] It had always been exploited by people living in or around them for millennia[174] and provides a wide range of benefits at the local, regional or global levels.[175] Some of these benefits can only be realised if the forest is conserved in its natural state, that is, untouched or subjected to limited human intervention. Other benefits can be obtained by interfering with the forest through the exploitation of timber and non-timber forest product (NTFP). As an ecosystem it provides a variety of goods and services for sustainable livelihood such as shelter, food, medicine,

---

173 Mather A. S., Global Forest Resources, Belhven Press, London, 1992, p. 4.

174 Vabi, M. B and Tchamou, N., "A Farming Perspective to NWFP Exploitation in the Support Zone of the Korup National Park of Cameroon: Determining the Connection between the Household and the Forest," in Non-Wood Forest Products of Central Africa, Current Research Issues and Prospects for Conservation and Development, FAO, 1999, p. 171.

175 BHFP, The Montane Forest of the North-West Province, A Teacher's Guide, November 2002, pp. 7& 12; BHFP, "Community Forestry Seminar Series, Information Note no. 4, What Makes People Want to Have a Community Forest", October 2001, p. 1; F.A.O, A Frame Work for Analyzing Institutional Incentives in Community Forestry," TFP/FAO 1992, p. 111.

timber, building material, craft material and natural habitat for both man and wildlife.[176]

Ecologically forest controls erosion, provides rainfall and protects natural water bodies from drying up. Its serves as the earth's air purifier by reducing the amount of carbon dioxide in the atmosphere during photosynthesis. Forests, to local communities are of great importance for cultural practices and religious worships.[177]

As a natural resource, the 1994 Forestry Law focuses only on the protection of tangible as against intangible benefits of community forests whereas its tangible values are a function of the intangible. That is why the 2003 Maputo Convention has given a wide definition to "natural resources" as renewable resources, tangible and intangible, including soil, water, flora and fauna as well as non-renewable resources.[178] Uncontrolled exploitation of tangible benefits with disregard to the intangible does not augur well for sustainable forest management. That is why local communities (legal entities) are expected to present annual reports of their activities, based on which such exploitation can be judged and controlled by MINFOF for sustainable forest management. But this is rarely done.

The benefits derived from community forests will be examined within the background of those that are tangible and regulated by law and intangible not covered by the law nor provided in community forests simple management plans.

3.2: Tangible Benefits

These refer to those benefits derived from community forests which can be seen, touched and even appropriated. They include wood, non-timber forest products (NTFP) or non-wood forest products (NWFP) which refer to forest products other than timber. NTFP and NWFP will be

176 Winkelmolen, M. B., "L'éducation Environnementale: Une Question D'acquisition des Savoirs Complémentaires. Réflexion Sur Une Approche », in Bulletin Arbres, Forêts et Communautés Rurales. No. 15/16 Spécial Cameroun, Décembre 1998, p. 62; See also Huff, P. R and Pencore, M., "Case Study: Menominee Tribal Enterprises" (Monominee Resevertion, Wisconsin,USA) LTC, IES, January 1995, p. 8.

177 Chi, M. A., " Legal recognition of sacred forests in Cameroon: Giving customary communal ownership rights statutory tenure rights," in Bojang, F. et al (eds.) Natural Resource Tenure Systems and their Implication for Agriculture, Food security and Nature conservation in Africa, Nature and Faune, vol. 24. Issue 2, FAO, 2010, p.26.

178 Article v (1).

interchangeably used as the two groupings that most clearly describe the sector. The irrational exploitation of these products as discussed below is a clear indication that community forests sustainability is uncertain.

3.2.1: Wood or Timber Products

Forests provide wood which is the most versatile and ubiquitous products in human use. Wood is the main source of energy not only for rural people, where all cooking and most processing depend on fuelwood,[179] but also for many of the urban poor. About 15.000 million cubic meter of wood is harvested yearly world-wide for fuel, furniture, building etc[180] and Africa accounts for more than one-quarter of global wood fuel production.[181] In Cameroon the total annual round wood production between 2005-2009 is estimated at about 14 million m3, of which 9.5-12 million m3 is fuelwood.[182] More than 1.5 thousand million people use wood daily for maintaining essential level of warmth in the homes, and about 200 million people world-wide depend on wood for cooking their food.[183] Wood used for bioenergy production increased from 2 billion cubic metres in 1970 to 2.6 billion cubic metres in 2005. This suggests that up to 3.8 billion cubic metres of wood would be required by 2030.[184]

Wood is the most important product, obtained from forests by village communities to meet energy needs. Studies conducted in the following communities show that 80-90% of the people rely on wood for cooking and several other activities such as brewing, smelting etc: Mindourou,[185] Beul, Mayos, and Petit Pol,[186] Ngola, Achip,[187] and Andjouk[188], in the East Region. Simbane,[189] Nkolevodo,[190] Vela[191] in the Centre Region. In the South West

---

179 Ndenecho, E. N., "Intergrating the livelihoods of forest-adjacent communities in forest conservation projects: Case study of mount Oku, Cameroon," in Journal of Applied Social Sciences, vol. 6, no. 1&2, University of Buea, Cameroon, 2007, p. 66.

180 www.focusonforests.org/fcontent/matter.htm (consulted 11 April, 2011); See also Biggs, D. " Forest Industry" Microsoft student 2009, who states that about 50% of wood harvested worldwide each year is used directly as fuel for heating and cooking.

181 FAO, State of the world's forest 2009, FAO, Rome, 2009, p. 6.

182 ITTO, Status of Tropical Forest Management 2011, Technical Series 38, June 2011, p. 51.

183 www.fao.org/docrep/t0692e/t (accessed 9/4/2011); See also FAO, Trees for Life 1991, p. 11.

184 www.scribd.com/doc/50402965/9/global-demand-for-wood-product (last consulted 05/04/2011).

185 This is a village in Dja Sub-Division.

186 These are villages in Dimako Sub-Division.

187 These villages are found in Lomie Sub-Division.

188 This is a village in Angossas Sub-Division.

189 This is a village in Nkoteng Sub-Division.

190 This is a village in Batchenga Sub-Division.

191 This is a village in Minta Sub-Division.

Region, they were Bimbia Bonadikombo in Limbe Sub-Division, Tinto in the Upper Bayang Sub-Division, Ndissi and Ekeb villages in Tombel Sub-Division and Manyemen in Nguti Sub-Division. In the South Region, Kondebilong in Zoetélé Sub-Division, Ndoundou in Bengbis Sub-Division, and Ngam in Sangmelima Sub-Division, while in the Littoral Region we have Nkokom in Yabassi Sub-Division, Boomaboong and Pouth-Djock in Edea Sub-Division.

Because Simple Management Plans (SMPs) of legal entities managing forests do not limit the volume or quantity of fuelwood to be exploited from the forests, uncontrolled exploitation of fuelwood could lead to community forest degradation, as was the case in Laikom community in the North West Region. To redress this situation, the forestry administration has embarked on reforestation. Local community preference for fuelwood is not only based on its energy but also on the belief that food cooked with firewood is more tasteful than that cooked with other source of energy.[192] The collection of dead wood, logging of life trees and eventually the uprooting of stumps and removal of shrubs to meet fuel needs leads to degradation of the forest.

Wood is used for furniture and several other industrial and domestic uses, such as fiber boards, mortar, chip boards, paper, cardboards etc. All houses within the forest communities in Cameroon are constructed with material gathered from the forests. Products such as rattan canes used for the making of furniture are collected from the forest. More trees are frequently felled with the help of chainsaw machines to produce weather-boarding for house construction and canoes for river transportation.

Economically, the cost of wood is rising.[193] World's demand for wood and wood products has been growing at the rate of one to two percent per year over the past decade.[194] Wood products are worth US $36.000 million per year, almost US $ 10.000 million of which comes from developing countries,[195] and Cameroon made about 320 billion FCFA (US $ 650 million) in 2004.[196] Cameroon is classified as the tenth largest tropical

---

[192] Belief affirmed by one lady from the North in "Hello" programme, C.R.T.V, Monday 12th February 2008, 6:20 am.

[193] Krsmer, J. T., "The Importance of Wood" available at www.kramer.org/whywood.htlm (last consulted on 9/07/2011).

[194] www.fao.org/docrep/to829e/to829E05.htm (accessed on 11/4/2011).

[195] Ibid.

[196] ITTO, Status of Tropical Forest Management 2011,Technical Series 38, June 2011, p.52.

timber exploiter in the world and the second in Africa after Gabon[197] and some of this wood come from community forests within countries of the Congo Basin.

Timber exploitation or logging in community forests just as in other classified forest is regulated and is discussed in chapter six. These include sale of standing volume, exploitation permits and individual felling authorisation. Unfortunately local communities are unable to distinguish the differences between these titles as was the case with NDECUDA[198] and REPA.[199] Because of government's lack of control, degradation rather than sustainable management of community forests is apparent.

3.2.2: Non-Timber Forest Products

These include wild plants and animals found in the forest once the main source of food for many early hunter societies. Forests and trees contribute directly to food security, providing fruits such as *irvingia gabonensis* (bush mangoes), nuts such as *garcina kola* (bitter kola), coconut, monkey kola and a variety of fish and bush meat collected from community forests and often eaten raw by some pygmy communities.[200]

Other edible foods such as *ricinodendrom heudeloti* (njangsanga), mushroom, and honey which play important roles in human nutrition, wild leaves such as *gnetum africanum* (eru) either fresh or dried, as well as seeds and nuts found in the forest are some of the most widely eaten forest foods gathered from community forests haphazardly. These products do not only constitute important traditional diets in many parts of Africa, and Latin America[201] especially within the local communities, but are also largely commercialised at both national and international levels. Though local population are suppose to exercise their rights of use, the collection of these products for commercial purpose seem to supersede their collection for local consumption. The result is the non respect of community forests SMPs and the lack of control by the forestry administration only goes to aggravate this process.

---

197 Ibid, p.51.

198 This is the legal entity managing a community within Ndissi and Ekeb villages in Tombel Sub-Division.

199 This is the legal entity managing a community in Manyemen within Nguti Sub-Division.

200 Interview with, Ndokoa, traditional ruler of the Mayos, 2009.

201 FAO, Common Forest Resource Management. Annoted Bibliography of Asia, Africa, and Latin America. FTP-FAO, 1993, p. 198.

The forest is widely valued as a source of medicinal plants. As stated by Tamajong about 80% of the world's population relies chiefly on traditional medicine which ingredients are derived from the forest.[202] Some local communities such as GIC COPAL have only one health centre for 10 villages[203] and Nkokom has no health centre and totally depends on traditional medicine.[204] The uncontrolled gathering of medicinal plants from these forests is evident due to the non respect of SMPs and the absence of administrative control. This state of affairs will certainly lead to the extinction of some endemic species which ought to be protected to enhance the ecological functioning of community forests.

However in some community forests such as those within Kilum/ Ijim mountain forest there are well organised forest-user groups of hunters, carvers, grazers, and traditional healers that existed before the advent of community forests. Traditional healers user-groups for instance, based on traditional knowledge regulated by their indigenous institutions manage and ensure the sustainable exploitation of medicinal plants. These products from the forest represent a source of medicine for 75-90% of people in developing countries and constitute the active ingredients found in 50% of prescription drugs.[205] Certain non-timber forest products (NTFP) such as palm and raffia used for the production of fiber for weaving, thatches for roofing, construction of houses, bridges, chairs[206] can be taped and consumed as beverages[207] or used as raw material for the production of other local alcoholic drinks such as "arki." The most common of such drink is "afofo" in Cameroon also known as "aquatshi" in Ghana.

Wildlife which constitutes NTFP found in the forest is illegally traded world-wide. According to Ofir, illegal trade in wildlife ranks third, after arms and drugs in the list of the world's most lucrative illegal trade

---

202 Tamajong, I., "Useful Plants of the Limbe Botanical Garden Nursery (Medicinal, Ornamental, Timber, Species) Botany Practical for the Decree Programme BSc Biology (Botany) University of Buea, 1995, p. 2.

203 SMP of COPAL, 2007, p. 13.

204 SMP of GIC DIPAN DI LONG, 2008, p. 8.

205 www.news.bbc.co.uk/2/hi/health/7196702.stm (last consulted on 06/04/2011).

206 Shiemo, N. P. "Economic Analyses of Raphia and Cane Products in Cameroon" A Dissertation in the Department of Forestry Resource Management Submitted to the Faculty of Agriculture and Forest in Partial Fulfillment of the requirement for the Decree of Masters of Science of the University of Ibadan. September 1982, pp. 28, 30 and 57.

207 Vabi, M. B and Tchamou, N (n 2) 175, where it is reported that tapping constitute an important supplementary income-generating activity to about 51% of the men in the Korup zone.

activities.[208] It plays a significant role in the diet of communities living around the forest. In some cases its even provides the single largest source of animal protein. The uncontrolled exploitation of wildlife within some community forests has an adverse impact on the sustainability of the forest. Exploitation is carried out with the use of guns, cutlasses, spears, traps or even pursuit which reduce the number of certain animal species such as elephants sometimes called "forest gardeners." This is because seeds are propagated through elephant droppings and regeneration of young plants takes place. The protection of wildlife is not certain because rules against hunting are flouted to the extent that a minimum of 2000 traps could be found in one area. The Tinto community forest covering 1295 hectares, where other animal species such as monkeys, duikers, porcupines, pigs and the like, including protected species are hunted, is a good example.[209]

3.2.3: Forest as Habitat

World forest and woodland provides dwelling places for more than 3000 million people[210] and for more than 200 million people in the tropics.[211] For instance more than 50.000.000 tribal people such as the Pygmies in central Africa, the Huli in the highland forest of Papua New Guinea (PNG) and the Yanomami in South America live permanently in the forest.[212] An estimated number of 100 to 300 million people live on edges of forest and use forest products for most of their daily needs.[213] This includes indigenous people as well as settlers and squatters and people who live part-time in the forest, working as small scale loggers, harvesters of forest products or using the forest as a place of refuge. For instance Bamenda Highlands Forest Project (BHFP) states that, during the Southern Cameroon Incident in 1997 many people hid themselves in the forest for weeks where they were able to meet their needs in terms of shelter, food, water and the like.[214]

Trees mitigate the excesses of sun, rain and temperature. They take the brunt of these elements and consequently lessen the impact of sun,

[208] Ofir, D., "Wildlife law enforcement wakes up!" in Wildlife Justice No. 002, LAGA, Yaounde, 2006, p. 2.
[209] Tinto Clan C F, Simple Management Plan, 2002.
[210] www.fao.org./docrep/t0692e/t (accessed April 11, 2011).
[211] www.fao.org./docrep/t0829e/To829E05.htm (last consulted 09/04/2011).
[212] www.srl.caltech.edu/personnwl/krubal/rainforest/edit560s6 (accessed April 02, 2011).
[213] www.focusonforests.org/fcontent/matter.htm (accessed April 15, 2011).
[214] BHFP, Community Forestry Seminar Series. Information note no. 3, Visit to the Kedjem Mawes forest to see how people use and manage their forest, October 2001, p. 1.

rainfall and reduce the vagaries of temperature change and take the punch out of strong winds forming a protective canopy, under which both man and animal may take refuge. The above mentioned comfort is certainly the reason why CADBAP (Communauté Active pour le Déveoppement des Bakoum, Baka et Pol) community forest is home for the pygmy population within Beul, Mayos and Petit Pol communities in the East Region. The forest does not only provide dwelling for human beings but equally provides ecosystem services to guarantee the livelihood of the communities, such as clean water supply and fresh air. Forest is also home to biodiversity and hosts about two-third of world's terrestrial species.[215] Forest serves as windbreaks, protects livestock, particularly young animals against the damaging effects of both cold and hot winds.[216]

Apparently the uncontrolled exploitation of community forests will not guarantee these important roles due to the ignorance of the local communities and lack of administrative controls.

3.2.4: Forests as Source of Income

For many communities the money derived from the collection, sale and processing of forest products provides essential input to the family income. The products derived from the forest for market purposes vary depending on the region, the market and local traditions.[217] Thus a rational management of forests resources will reduce illegal and informal trade in forest products,[218] since members of the community will serve as forests guards and trap down illegal exploiters. This will certainly reduce illegal trade in wildlife which as mentioned earlier ranks third after arms and drugs in the list of the world's most lucrative international illegal trade activities.[219]

---

215 www.fao.org/docrep/fao/011/i0350eo2apdf (accessed April 05, 2011).

216 www.forestmonitory.org (last consulted 06/04/2011).

217 In the villages around the Korup national park in Cameroon, hunting constitutes the single source of income for many households, and averagely hunters earn proximally 350.000 FCFA per annum which accounts for about 38% of the total village income. In the Ashante region in Ghana, it is rather the collection of food wrapping leaves which constitutes the major source of income in some villages.

218 Ladipo, D. O., "The Development of Quality Control Standards for Ogbono (*Irvingia Gabonensis* and *irivingia Wombolu*) Kernels: Efforts towards Encouraging Organised and Further International Trade in a NWFP of the West and Central Africa," in Non-Wood Forest Products of Central Africa. Current Research Issues and Prospects for Conservation and Development. FAO, 1999, p. 245.

219 Speech draft by the Minister of Forestry and Wildlife, His Excellency Egbe Achuo Hillman on the Occasion of the Signing of a Memorandum of Understanding (MOU) between the Government of Cameroon and the Last Great Ape Organisation (LAGA); See also Kam Yogo, E. D., « Les Etats Africains face à la protection des éléphants d'Afrique par le droit international de l'environnement », in Juridis Périodique. Revue de Droit et de Sciences Politiques No. 57, Yaounde, 2004, p. 81.

Forests also generate income through ecotourism,[220] which is tourism that has as its primary purpose an interaction with nature.[221] Ecotourism does not only promote the involvement of local communities in forest management but makes important contributions to the economic development of many developing countries. As a touristic site, the forest serves as a means of acquiring foreign currency and enhances international prestige. For instance Bimbia Bonadikombo Natural Resource Management Council[222] (BBNRMC) in the year 2007 and 2008 generated the sum of 395.000 FCFA and 125.000 FCFA, respectively, from tourism.[223] However as stated by Koziel, increasing number of visitors and intensity of tourist activities can rather degrade the natural environment.[224] This can be through frequent interaction in some ecological sensitive areas that may lead to the migration of some species of fauna and the destruction of some species of flora.

Other resources derived from the forest that generates income include edible products and craft material for the production of furniture, baskets, mat and other products from cane, reeds and vines which are sold locally or internationally. The forestry sector in Cameroon comes second after petroleum in term of revenue generation. It accounts for 11% of the country's gross domestic product (GDP) and 20% of its export trade. Forest in Cameroon also contributes over 40 billion FCFA to the country's revenue[225] and accounts for over 40.000 jobs[226] in 2005 and 45.000 in 2010.[227] For instance BBNRMC employed local people to serve as forest guards. This employment was nevertheless short-live since the legal entity charged with the management of this community forest was unable to pay these guards.

The gathering of NTFP equally constitutes a source of employment to most communities. Hunting for instance which is the oldest human

---

220 Pontes, S. S., "The Forest Resource and Its Importance in Sao Tome and Principe" in Cleaver, K. et al., (eds.) Conservation of West and Central African Rainforest, WBEP, no. 1, Washington D.C USA, 1992, p. 40.

221 Koziel, E and Saunders, J., (eds) Living off Biodiversity. Exploring Livelihoods and Biodiversity Issues in Natural Resource Management, NRI, IIED, London, 2001, p. 43.

222 This is the legal entity managing the community forest within Bonakikombo, Bonabile, Bonagombe, Liwanda and Dikilo villages.

223 BBNRMC, 2007 and 2008 Annual Reports.

224 Koziel (n 49).

225 The Herald News Paper no. 1678 Monday 8-9 August 2005, p. 12.

226 Ibid; See also Besong, J. B., "New Directions in National Forestry Policies-Cameroon," in Conservation of West and Central African Rainforest. WBEP, no. 1, p. 36;

227 ITTO (n 10) 53.

activity within the Manyemen community constitutes the principal source of income for many households. It is the only activity for which people from neighbouring community are involved. Fishing within this community is also a source of employment. Women fish in streams (Ngang and Basong) closer to the village while men concentrate in rivers (Manyu, Mbu Mfi) found in the forest. 90% of the catch is consumed locally while 10% is sold within the community.[228] Within the community forest managed by *ATOTENA de MEBEM* (GIC ATEM), traditional fishing generates about 500.000 to 1000.000 yearly.[229] As much as 450.000 FCFA per month is said to have been made from the sale of *gnetum africanum* commonly known as *eru* by one full time trader in the product in the Idenau market in 1997, and it was estimated that 600 tons of *eru*, some from community forests with a market value of 1800 000 000 FCFA leave this market yearly.[230]

Also international trade in rattan alone is currently worth some US $6.5 billion a year, with a majority of the trade concentrating on species of Asian origin.[231] In Tanzania for instance, over 5000 people mostly men are engaged in charcoal production for energy as their only source of income. This number represents over 8% of the economically active population of that country.[232] In Cebu, Philippines, it is estimated that fuelwood and charcoal production provides supplemental employment and income to at least 35.000 rural families or 15% of the population.[233] In Pakistan, over 85.000 people are employed in charcoal and fuelwood production while in Addis Ababa, Ethiopia more than 10.000 women and children rely on feulwood gathering and sale as a principal source of earnings.[234] It was even discovered that in Kenya charcoal makers earn 2.5 times the official farm wage, while charcoal producers around Pokhara in Nepal earned 2.5 times the wage rate of labouring in a construction industry.[235] Unfortunately

---

[228] SMP, Tinto community forest, 2002.

[229] Interview with, Bidima Angoua Daniel, FMO of GIC ATEM, 2009.

[230] Shiembo, N. S., "The Sustainability of Eru (*Gnetum Africanum* and *Gnetum Buchholzianum*): Over Exploited Non-Wood Forest Products From the Forests of Central Africa," in Non-Wood Forest Products of Central Africa, Current Research Issues and Prospects for Conservation and Development. FAO, 1999, p. 62.

[231] Sunderland, T. C. H. "Recent Research into African Rattans (*Palmae*): A Valuable Non-Wood Forest Product from the Forests of Central Africa," in Non-Wood Forest Products of Central Africa, Current Research Issues and Prospects for Conservation and Development. FAO, 1999, p. 87.

[232] Townson, I. M., "Forest Products and Household Income." A Review of Annotated Bibliography, OFI/CIFOR, 1995, p. 4.

[233] Ibid.

[234] Ibid.

[235] Ibid.

one of the key problems in assessing the financial contribution of African forests is the absence of reliable information even in the case of marketed goods.[236]

3.3: Intangible Benefits

These are ecosystem services rendered to humanity by all forests. These benefits can neither be seen nor touched but their effects are felt by humanity as a whole. The availability of intangible benefits depends on the conservation of tangible benefits. The irrational and uncontrolled exploitation of wood and NWFP from community forests will negatively affect intangible services derived from these forests such as hydrology (water), soil protection and global climate regulation etc.

3.3.1: Effects of Deforestation on Hydrology

The uncontrolled and irrational exploitation of wood and timber from community forests as discussed earlier will adversely affect water availability. In Cameroon for instance mean annual rainfall per month has decreased by about 2.9 mm (2.2%) per decade since 1960 and the country experienced low rainfall between 2003 and 2006.[237] Trees through ecosystem services supply fresh and potable water which is an important motivation for population settlement and livelihood.[238] The need for portable water was one of the objectives of the Kilum-Ijim project in creating community forests in the North-West Region of Cameroon. Water insecurity contributed to the out-break of cholera in the northern regions of the country and gradually extending to other part of the country.

The role of forest as providing water was certainly the reason why in resolving conflict over the ownership of Laikom Community forest, the forestry administration allowed the people to cultivate the forestland while they carry out reforestation by planting trees on the cultivated areas. The local community was asked not to tamper with the trees so as to guarantee constant water supply. The role of forest as water provider is equally shared by Nizar, who states that in Ivory Coast, the flow of rivers is higher in

---

236 FAO, Forestry Outlook Study for Africa. Regional Report-Opportunities and Challenges Towards 2020. FAO Forestry Paper 141, Rome, 2003, p. 8.

237 ITTO, Status of Tropical Forest Management 2011,Technical Series 38, June 2011, p. 47.

238 Lambi, C. M "The Difficult Life of the Kridi: The Mandara mountain Settlement of North Cameroon" in Lambi, C. M and Eze, E. B (eds) A Reading in Geography. UPCA, Bamenda, Cameroon, 2001, p. 399.

natural forests than in coffee plantations during the dry season.[239] It was equally discovered in Malaysia that the flow of rivers from primary forests roughly double those from rubber and oil plantations.[240] Notwithstanding, the importance attached to forest as water provider, some authors argue that the function of forests as increasing rainfall as well as watershed are simply forest myths.[241]

3.3.2: Impact of Forest Clearance on Soil Protection

Clearing the forest may cause changes in the physical and chemical characteristics of the soil, resulting to leaching or water induced soil erosion. Redmond is of the opinion that water induced erosion deposits about 3.5 million tons of eroded material into the oceans yearly.[242] Serving as wind breaks and shelterbelts, forests reduce wind speed and protect land from wind erosion up to a distance of at least 20 times their heights.[243] Forest conservation will protect the land area from inundation and physical damage while its destruction will cause landslides, increase flooding and degrade drinking water. In the Himalayas, for instance, deforestation is responsible for the annual flooding of 409 million hectares in India and washes away millions of tons of silt into the Bangladesh River each year.[244] It is expected that within Laikom Community Forest reforestation practiced will prevent landslides and soil erosion.

3.3.3: Consequences of Deforestation on Global Climate

Two notable ways in which forests influences the global climate change are through, reflected heat from land and the level of carbon dioxide (CO2) in the atmosphere. Climate change refers to short, medium and long term changes in weather patterns and temperature that are predicted to happen or are already happening as a result of the emission of greenhouse gases such as CO2 altering world's temperature and seasonal variation. Some gases in the atmosphere such as CO2 trap heat which would otherwise be radiated into space.[245] The impact this has on global

---

[239] Nizar, M. and Keven, G., "Forestry on Customary owned land: Some experience from south Pacific," O.D.I Working Paper 19a, 1996, p. 217.
[240] Ibid.
[241] FAO, The Challenge of Sustainable Forest Management : What Future for the world's Forests? FAO Publication, 1993, p. 44.
[242] Redmond, W. A., "Erosion." Microsoft® Studen Corporation, Encarta 2009.
[243] FAO, Trees for life, 1991, p. 20.
[244] FAO, Forestry and Food Security, 1989, p. 20.
[245] FAO (n 71) 42.

heat balance has become a cause for wide spread concerned, evidenced in the signing of the Montreal Protocol in September 1987 on substances that depletes the ozone layer.

Forests form a close canopy which absorbs more solar radiation than any other vegetation type and reflects less heat in the atmosphere. The fraction of reflected radiation is known as "albedo." The removal of community forests through uncontrolled and irrational exploitation of timber may result in the increase of "albedo" causing global warming. It has even been reported that the global temperature of the earth increased from 0.3° C to 0.6° C in the 20th Century.[246] Balling suggests that, the world temperature may approach 10° C from coldest to warmest periods.[247] In Cameroon the mean annual temperature has increased by 0.7° C since 1960 at an average rate of increase of 0.15° C per decade.[248]

Since trees and green plants absorb CO_2 during photosynthesis, preservation, reforestation and sustainable management of community forests could counter the increase in greenhouse gases in the atmosphere. "Albedo" could therefore be reduced by incorporating the protection of intangible benefits in the SMPs of community forests. It is true that the sustainable management of tangible benefits indirectly incorporates the sustainability of ecosystem services. Nevertheless we submit that the sustainability of intangible services will be better enhanced if direct reference is made to them in the SMPs of community forests or the management agreements.

3.3.4: Deforestation Erode Local Cultures

Community forests to local or indigenous people have both aesthetic and decorative functions.[249] The irrational and uncontrolled exploitation of these forests leads to the destruction of local cultures and traditions contrary to the spirit of article 8 (j) of the 1992 CBD. The community forests within the Kilum/Ijim site houses sacred place where

---

246 Tsayem M. D., « Caractérisation et suivi de la Déforestation en Milieu Tropical par Télédétection. Application aux Défrichements Agricoles en Guyane Française et Brésil. » Thèse de docteur de L'université D'Orléans, 2002, p. 23.

247 Balling, B. "The increase in Global Temperature: What it doers and does not tell us," available at www.marshall.org//pdf/matreials/170.pdf (accessed on 08/04/2011).

248 ITTO (10) 47.

249 Abou, B. A. B. K. et al., Islamic Principles for the Conservation of Natural Environment. IUCN Switzerland, 1983, p. 16.

sacrifices, religious and cultural rites are performed.[250] In Oku community, when a new Fon is enthroned he has to move round the Oku Lake found in the forest as part of his enthronement ritual.[251] In Kom when a Fon is enthroned he has to be taken to the Laikom community forest for some rituals. Portions of forests such as groves in which the leaders of the villages are buried are even reserved for individual use by traditional rulers. These places are sacred and protected because of the reverence for dead chiefs and the belief that forests constitute not only a home for ancestral spirits, but also for the spirits of the living.

The exposure of these sacred places through uncontrolled timber exploitation destroys indigenous cultures which protection ought to have been re-enforced with the advent of community forests. If government had chosen the right parties in the management of community forests, local cultures would have been protected and forest sustainability ensured through indigenous institutions.

In some communities, the use of certain trees is forbidden by indigenous customs because of the magical value they are believed to possess. For instance, the Gabra in Kenya do not allow *salvadora persica* (a tree species) to be used as fuelwood, for these species are reserved only for the making of religious artefacts. The Garahwali communities in India worship *Bhumidevata* (a tree) to signify their veneration of land and nature,[252] while in Thailand sacred forests are reserved mainly for ceremonial purposes with the belief that these forests are inhabited by spirits.[253] In Cameroon also, the initiation ceremonies of the Fang in the southern part of the country are always held at the base of a large tree that symbolises the forest, which houses the body of god.[254] As a matter of fact, land and forest throughout Cameroon and Africa "has religious or supernatural significance as here tribal or family ancestors are buried on the land, or the land is itself a deity which requires placating."[255] Binet, J., noted

---

250 Kabuye, C., "Socio-Economic Research and Non-Wood Forest Products: An Overview," in Non-Wood Forest Products of Central Africa, Current Research Issues and Prospects for Conservation and Development. FAO, 1999, p. 114.

251 BHFP (n 42).

252 ODA's Review of Participatory Forest Management, Synthesis of Findings, August 1996, p. 3.

253 Ganjanapan, A., "The Politics of Conservation and the Complexity of Local Control of Forests in the Northern Thai highlands," in Mountain Research and Development vol. 18, no 1, UCP, February 1998, p. 78.

254 FAO (n 72) 13.

255 cf. Anyangwe, C., "Land Tenure and Interests in Land," in Cameroon Law Review, 2nd series Nr 27, 1984, p. 35.

that *le sol apparaît comme un usufruit confié aux hommes par les divinités*[256] and Delarozière stated categorically that *la terre est en relation étroite avec les aïeux de la tribu.*[257] This implies that there is a close relation between the land including forest and the gods or ancestors of the community.

The veneration of forest or part thereof by local customs would be reason enough to suggest that community forests would be better managed by the use of local customs, than by government created entities, with imposed management rules.

3.4: Conclusion

Community forests are important to local communities. They provide tangible and intangible benefits such as wood and non-wood products, serve as habitat and gives opportunities for many income generating activities. They equally provide ecosystem services such as soil conservation, regulating water supply, and climate change and serve in the conservation of local cultures.

The irrational and uncontrolled exploitation of community forests does not guarantee the attainment of the above cited benefits. The non-respect of SMPs of community forests as is the case with virtually all community forests will result in an over exploitation of NTFP. The enthusiasm expressed by indigenous people in the proper management of sacred forest make them best placed to ensure community management of forests.

---

256 Ibid.

257 Ibid.

CHAPTER FOUR

STAKEHOLDERS PROMOTING THE INTEGRATION OF INDIGENOUS COMMUNITY IN THE MANAGEMENT OF ENVIRONMENTAL RESOURCES

4.0: Introduction

Section 37 (1) of the 1994 Forestry Law provides that:

> The services in charge of forests shall in order to promote the management of forest resources by village communities which so desire, give them assistance. An agreement shall then be signed between the two parties. The technical assistance thus given to the village communities shall be free of charge.

Article 3 (11) of the 1995 Forestry Decree stipulates that:

> A community forest: a forest of the non-permanent State forest, object of a management agreement between a village community and the service in charge of forest. The management of such a forest shall be the responsibility of the village community concerned, with the technical assistance of the service in charge of forestry.

As could be deduced from the above provisions, parties competent to sign community forests management agreements are government on the one hand and local community on the other. These stakeholders, referred to as direct actors, do not only have an interest in the acquisition, management and exploitation of community forests and their resources,[258] but equally have a socio-anthropological, legal and institutional link with the forests.[259] They are usually assisted by other actors such as NGOs in the creation or management of community forests.

It is argued that local communities are endowed with traditional or customary institutions. The problem here deals with recognition of these existing customary institutions or adopting those provided by the law[260] defined as legal entities. The implication is that the latter have replaced the former in the management of community forests. Conversely the Forestry Law ought to empower indigenous institutions such as Chiefs, Fons, Lamidos etc which the people obey and respect and which in practical terms government utilises in community forest management, rather than creating legal entities (Associations, CIG, EIG and Cooperative Societies) which objectives are not related to forest conservation. For example CIG just as cooperative societies are organisations of economic and financial nature set up voluntarily by individuals having common interest and working together as a group.[261] They are not endowed with the required indigenous knowledge nor are their practices suited to represent local communities to participate in the management of community forest as recommended by the 1992 Convention on Biological Diversity (CBD). Article 8 (j) of that convention clearly states that "each contracting party shall ... respect, preserve and maintain knowledge...and practices of indigenous and local communities" and is echoed in article 1 of the 2005 COMIFAC Treaty which calls on member States to "step up efforts to increase the rapid participation of rural populations in the planning and sustainable management of ecosystems and allot adequate areas for their socio-economic development".

258 NRI, "Trees Resources and Environmental Policy: A stakeholder Approach," NRI Socio-Economic Series7, NRI-ODA, 1994, p. vi.

259 Fouda, Y. and Bigombe, P. L., « Les Acteurs Environnementaux au Cameroun: Etat des Lieux. » GTZ, Octobre 2000, p. 7.

260 See article 28 (3) of the 1994 Forestry Decree.

261 See article 49 of Law no. 92/006 of 14/08/1992 relating to Co-operative Societies and Common Initiative Groups.

4.1: Government as Principal Stakeholder

The government is represented by the Ministry of Forestry and Wildlife (MINFOF) and the decentralised services of the Ministry of Territorial Administration and Decentralisation (MINATD) in the Regions and Divisions as one of the principal parties qualified to sign community forests Management Agreements. Article 27 (3) of the Forestry Decree states that:

> ...the agreement shall be signed as the case may be, by:
>
> (a) The Divisional Officer where the forest concerned falls within the jurisdiction of the Division;
>
> (b) The Governor where the forest concerned spans two Divisions of the Province;
>
> The Minister in charge of forestry, where the forest concerned spans two Provinces.

It is evident from the above provision that it is the duty of MINFOF where the forest concerned spans two or more Regions to sign the management agreements with the local communities as another principal party. The management agreement is signed by the Governor or the SDO if the forest concerned spans two or more Divisions of the Region and if the forest in question comes within one Division, respectively. Government as one of the principal actor in signing community forests management agreement is not only peculiar to Cameroon. In Guatemala, the management agreement known as "concession contract" is signed between the local community and National Parks Authority which is a government department.[262] In India local communities equally sign management agreement with the Forestry Department while in Gambia the community signs a preliminary community forest management agreement with government.[263]

In conformity with the Forestry Law, a cross section of community forests within our study site had their Management Agreements signed by their various S.D.Os since none of the forests under consideration

[262] Long, C., Forest and Community control: Official process that permits formal recognition of community management and rights and their relevance to the Democratic Republic of Congo, IIED, 2010, p. 8.

[263] Ibid pp. 13 & 17.

spanned beyond a Division. For instance the Management Agreements (MA) of the Association *Communauté Active pour le Déveoppement des Bakoum, Baka et Pol* (CADBAP) and that of Groupe *d'Initiative Commune des Jeunes Agriculteurs D'Andjouk* (GIC JAGRA) found in the East Region were signed in 2008. The agreement effectively signed by the President of *GIC JAGRA* and the SDO for Haut Nyong has no reference number and the name of the SDO who signed the agreement is not mentioned. The Management Agreements of *GIC DIPAN DI LONG* (DI DI LO) and *Boomaboong and Pouth-Njock* (GIC BOPO) both found in the Littoral Region were signed on the 20th of December 2002 (without a reference number) and 22nd of June 2007 respectively. *Groupe d'Initiatve Commune des Agriculteur de Ngam II*, (GICAM) in the Center Region had its Management Agreement signed without a reference number on the 29th of October and Tinto Clan CF, a common imitative group found in the South-West Region had theirs equally signed without a reference number on the 3rd of December 2002. Rural Environmental Poverty and Alleviation Common Initiative Group (REPA GIC) found in the South-West Region signed its Management Agreement without a reference number on the 19th March 2008, and the Association of Bimbia Bonadikombo Natural Resource Management Council (BBNRMC) equally situated in the South-West Region signed on the 18th of May 2002.[264] Most of the documents are devoid of reference numbers and names of the signing authorities; and this put to question their authenticity and validity.

4.2: Local Community

Here we are comparing existing indigenous institutions created by local communities such the chiefs and sacred societies (e.g. kwihfon) with those provided by the 1994 Forestry Law such as Common Initiative Group (CIG also referred to by it French acronym as GIC), Economic Interest Groups (EIG), Associations and Cooperative Societies[265] supposedly imposed by government and foreign to local communities. The chapter will compare these modern with indigenous institutions to highlight their relevance in the management of community forests (see table 4.1).

---

264 Management Agreement of Bimbia Banadikombo community forest, No. 1101/77.

265 See section 3.1 of the 2009 Manual of Procedures for the Attribution, and Norms for the Management of Community Forests.

TABLE 4.1 MODERN AND INDIGENOUS INSTITUTIONS COMPARED

INSTITUTIONS	OBJECTIVES	LOCATION	REFERENCES
MODERN - Association (mostly cultural)	Regroup members of various backgrounds to promote solidarity.	Mostly urban areas	law no. 90/53 of 19 December 1990 on Freedom of Associations
- Common Initiative Groups	Promote private economic and financial initiatives.	Same as above	Law no. 92/006 of 14 August 1992 on Co-operative and Common Initiative Groups Decree no. 92/445/PM of 23 November 1992 on Cooperative Societies and EIG
- Cooperative Societies	Commercialisation of members' products and distribution of profits.	Same as above	Same as above
Economic Interest Groups	Facilitate, develop and ameliorate economic and financial activities of members.	Same as above	Law no. 93/015 of 12 December 1993 on Economic Interest Groups OHADA Uniform Act on Commercial Companies and Economic Interest Groups January 1, 1998.
INDIGENOUS - Chiefs or Fons	Classified as leaders of village communities.	Rural areas	Decree No. 77/245 of July 1977 on the Organisation of Chiefdoms.

Sacred Societies	Legislate village norms.	Same as above	Important traditional organs of village Organisation
User groups	Manage specific NTFP	Same as above	Based on interest and know-how in sustainable use of NTFP

Source: author

As the table above shows, it will be noticed that there is a big difference between modern and indigenous institutions based on their objectives, location and the dates of their creation, as explained below.

4.2.1: Objectives of Institutions

As could be deduced from the table above the institutions are both modern and indigenous. The objectives of legal entities (modern institutions) set by the 1994 Forestry Law for the management of community forests do not tie with the objectives of community forests. Community forest are principally aimed at reducing or preventing forest resource degradation through the use of indigenous or cultural practices, enabling local community to have secure access to, and ownership of, the resource and their benefits. Community forest also aims at environmental protection through forest conservation and enhanced wildlife management.[266] But Associations, Cooperative societies, CIGs and EIGs are driven by motives of making and distributing profits to their members. It is worth noting that the principal activity of a Cooperative society and a CIG is the commercialisation of members' product which is incompatible with the objectives of community forests. The 1992 law on Cooperative society and CIG states that:

> The distribution of annual profits, after the appropriation for the statutory reserve fund has be made, shall be determined by the annual general meeting on the recommendation of the board of directors. Bonuses distributed or accredited to

[266] Bojang F., "Overview of International Workshop on Community Forestry in Africa" in Proceedings of International Workshop on Community Forestry in Africa. Participatory Forest Management a Strategy for Sustainable Forest Management in Africa, Gambia, 26-30 April, 1999, p. 9.

> members shall be proportional to the number of transactions made by each of them with the cooperative society.[267]

This implies that the distribution of profits or bonuses to members of a Cooperative society depend on the volume of transaction made by the member. Article 2 of the 1993 law on EIG and article 869 of the OHADA Uniform Act (UA) on Commercial Companies and Economic Interest Groups all stress the fact that this entity is aimed at facilitating, developing and ameliorating the economic activities of its members. The Uniform Act (UA) in it article 869 for instance provides that:

> An Economic Interest Group shall be one which has the exclusive object of putting in place for a specified duration all the means necessary to facilitate or develop the economic activities of its members and to improve or increase income from the said activity. Its activity shall mainly be connected with the economic activity of its members and shall not be of an auxiliary nature in relation thereto.

Associations are generally aimed at regrouping members of diverse background to promote solidarity. It is defined by the 1990 Law on Freedom of Associations:

> *L'Association est une convention par laquelle des personnes mettent en commun leurs connaissances ou leurs activités dans un but autre que de partager des bénéfices.*[268]

The objectives of modern entities are incompatible with those of community forests. A community forest is aimed at improving the socio economic condition of the entire village community alongside the sustainable management of forest resources. The difficulties in determining which of the legal entities meet the aspiration of community forests made the local people invariably chose one entity or the other for the management of their forests.

---

267 Articles 35 (1) and 11 of Law no. 92/006 of 14 August 1992 on Co-operative and Common Initiative Groups.

268 Article 2 of law no. 90/53 of 19 December 1990 on Freedom of Associations.

Out of a sample of about twenty-one supposed community forests, three are managed by Associations. These are Ndissi and Ekeb community forest managed by "Ndissi-Ekeb Cultural and Development Association" (NDECUDA) found in the South-West Region, Ngola Community Forest managed by an Association representing the Gbo, Pâ and Bamouh communities of Ngola and Achip (GBOBAPA) located in the East Region and lastly Bimbia Bonadikombo community forest managed by Bimbia Bonadikombo Natural Resource Management Council[269] (BBNRMC). One by a cooperative society, *Coopérative des Planteurs de la Léki*[270] (CO.PA.L) located in the Center Region, none by an EIG and the rest by Common Initiative Groups. A few examples are: Rural Environmental Poverty and Alleviation (REPA-CIG); *Force Vives Yembani Vela*[271] (GIC FOUYVE) in the Center Region; *Communauté Active pour le Déveoppement des Bakoum, Baka et Pol*[272] (CADBAP).

Modern entities are neither endowed nor able to make use of indigenous knowledge and practices to contribute in the management of community forests, whereas the law empowers and recognises traditional authorities in other domains such as:

> the competence to settle disputes relating to the use of some natural resources, especially water and pasture on the strength of local ways and customs, without infringing on the rights of the parties to the conflict to refer the matter to the competent court.[273]

From the above provision local institutions have the mandate to enforce regulations related to the use of water and forest resources for they have been instrumental in the management of these natural resources from time immemorial.

The Chiefs or Fons are leaders of village communities and have the duty to enforce customary rules that guarantee the sustainable management

---

[269] This Association was legalised on the 20th of November 1998.

[270] This legal entity was created on the 21st June 2001 and is registered under reference no. CE/CO/02/01/5839.

[271] See Registration certificate no. CE/GP/30/01/5697 signed on 23rd April 2001.

[272] See Registration no. 35/RDA/B13/BAPP.

[273] Article 93 of the 1996 Environmental Law; See also section 142 of the 1994 Forestry law which provides that before forestry official search houses within the community to detect criminals, they must consult traditional authorities.

of forests. Some traditional governing bodies such as kwihfon even enact village norms that regulate the exploitation of forest resources. For instance in the community forest within Kilum/Ijim certain portion of the forest are reserved for the use of traditional rulers thus limiting the influence and pressure of exploiters. There are equally village user groups with the objective of managing non-timber forest products (NTFP) sustainably. These groups are specialised in the management and exploitation of specific NTFP based on their interest and know-how in sustainable use of NTFP. Few examples are carvers, bee-farmers and medicinal plant collectors' user groups. The objectives of indigenous institutions, coupled with their location make them more apt in the management of these resources than modern entities.

The competence of local communities in the management of forest resources is well demonstrated in the management of sacred forests. These are areas of forestlands which are generally attached to the palaces of traditional rulers such as those of Kom, Oku and Bafut. They are considered sacred because they are believed to be home for the gods, the spirits of the dead and the living. Their sustainability and management is very effective due to the myths which endow the areas with a quality of sacredness. These myths prescribe dreadful diseases such as madness, illness leading to death or death likely to befall those who violate indigenous customs. An example by Dr. Chi is the case of one Ako and Amahbow who became mad because they without permission entered the Bafut sacred forest sanctuary to see the shrine.[274] Fear therefore sometimes serves as a *de-facto* forest conservation strategy, as customary rules are not abused to protect the forest. The foregoing suggest that community forests indigenous institutions have been marginalised by government in favour of modern institutions hitherto had never been involved in forest or natural resource management. This justifies the difficulties encountered in the establishment of community forests projects in the country.

4.2.2: Location of Institutions

As could be depicted from table 4.1, indigenous institutions are located within the local communities and are headed by traditional rulers who are accountable to its people, which is not the case with modern institutions. The latter are created indiscriminately in both rural and

[274] Chi, M. A., "Co-Management of Forest in Cameroon, The Compatibility of Government Policies with Indigenous Practices," Ph.D Thesis, Technology School, Maastricht, 1999, p. 55.

urban areas and are governed by executives elected by and represent only registered members. Unlike indigenous institutions members of modern institution do not necessarily share the same place of residence. This is one of the factors that accounts for the poor management of community forests within the country. For instance the FMO of Tinto clan community forest resides in Limbe, while that of DI DIPAN DI LONG is permanently resident in Douala and hardly visits the village.[275]

4.2.3: Creation of Institutions

Table 4.1 classifies the mode of creating the various institutions. Modern entities charged with the management of community forests were created in the 90s and follow a more or less complex procedure for their formation, whereas indigenous institutions exist from time immemorial and were only classified into first, second and third class chieftaincies.

Cooperative societies are governed by Law no. 92/006 of 14 August 1992 and Decree no. 92/445/PM of 23 November 1992. They are created at the Regional Delegation of Agriculture which may be time consuming and far from the local people, as compared to traditional institutions which do not need to be created and are found within the local communities. Co-operatives societies have a complex and cumbersome management structure, which may not respond to the participatory approach required for rural community natural resource management. The management organs of a co-operative include a General Assembly or an Assembly of Delegates, a Board of Directors, a Supervisory Committee, a Manager and an Audit Committee. These organs must meet the standard set by the Economic and Monetary Community of Central African States,[276] commonly known by its French acronym as CEMAC. The ruling organ of the local community is composed of the chief and the sacred society recognised and respected by all villagers, unlike cooperative societies which are recognised only by its registered members.

Economic Interest Groups were formally governed by Law no. 93/015 of 12 December 1993 on Economic Interest Groups, and legalised at the Court of First Instance of the area concerned. Today they are governed

[275] Interview with Tim David and Bataké Joseph, notables of Nkokom village , 2009.

[276] See generally articles 15-39 of Law no. 92/006 of 14 August 1992 on Co-operative and Common Initiative Groups.

by the OHADA Uniform Act on Commercial Companies and Economic Interest Groups and can be registered at the Registry of Commerce.[277] The UA further provides that:

> Two or more natural persons or corporate bodies, including persons exercising a liberal profession governed by a legislative or statutory instrument or whose title is protected, may form between them an economic interest group...[278]

The fact that an EIG can be created by two persons only, confirms the fact that it is not representative of the local community. A forest managed by such an entity cannot be considered as community forest because the royalties from such forest will be limited only to its members as ordained or provided by the law governing such an entity.

Like Cooperative societies, CIG are governed by Law no. 92/006 of 14 August 1992 and Decree no. 92/445/PM of 23 November 1992. The law stipulates that:

> Common initiative groups are organisation of an economic and financial nature set up voluntarily by individuals having common interests and working together as a group...formed by a declaration in writing during a constituent meeting of at least 5 (five) persons.[279]

A CIG is thus an entity of a social and economic nature established voluntarily by individuals having common interests and working together as a group. It is an entity that is easy to create, for as few as 5 persons can create a CIG by mere declaration during a constituent assembly. It is registered at the Regional Delegation of Agriculture and allows benefits to be distributed to members. The fact that the entity is registered only at the Regional headquarter constitutes a major constraint to communities that are enclaved or far away from their Regional capital. The requirement of 5 persons to create a CIG gives room for the creation of an entity that might

---

277 Article 872 of the UA provides that: "An Economic interest group shall have cooperate personality and full capacity with effect from registration in the Trade and Personal Property Credit Register."

278 Article 871 of UA on Commercial Companies and Economic Interest Group.

279 Article 49 and 50 of Law no. 92/006 of 14 August 1992 on Co-operative and Common Initiative Groups.

not be representative of the local community, thus contrary to the very idea of a community forest, which is supposed to be owned and managed by the entire village community.

Associations are governed by Law no. 90/53 of 19 December 1990 relating to Freedom of Associations. It is an entity easily created and managed. Although a prior formal constituent Assembly is required for the formation of an Association, it can nevertheless be created without a constituent general assembly of the founding members. All the law requires is for members to file an application or declaration at the SDO's office of the area where the Association's headquarter is located stating the name, purpose and headquarter of the Association. The application should also contain the names and signatures or thumb prints of members as well as the occupation and addresses of those responsible for running the Association. To the application or declaration must be attached two copies of the constitution, which must not contain provisions or envisage activities impairing national integration.[280]

> Article 11 of the 1990 law on freedom of Association equally states that:
> *Hormis les associations reconnues d'utilité publique, aucune association déclarée ne peut recevoir ni subventions des personnes publiques, ni dons et legs des personnes privées.*

Associations not recognized by Presidential Decree as serving public interest cannot receive public subsidies, gifts and legacies, and are prohibited from distributing benefits to members. Considering that communities will certainly be interested not only in distributing benefits to members but also in receiving public subsidies, gifts and legacies, Associations therefore are not the best entities for the acquisition and management of community forests.

It must be remarked that the procedure for the formation of any of the legal entities required for the management of community forests is not only cumbersome and time consuming but equally generates antagonism between the members and local communities; which impairs the efficient management of community forests.

[280] Se generally articles 6-8 of Law no. 90/53 of 19 December 1990 relating to Freedom of Associations.

4.3: Shortcomings of Modern Entities on Community Forests

The modern entities for the management of community forests rather generate conflicts than provide acceptable norms in the management of these forests. The negative effects of these entities could be deduced from the cloudy nature of their membership, the constant struggle for power between modern entities and local institutions, conflicts within the legal entity itself and with the forestry administration, lack of cooperation from indigenous and administrative authorities and misdirection of external support. These difficulties make the local people lack confidence in modern entities and rely more on their indigenous institutions which are indispensable in the sustainable management of forest resources.

4.3.1: Cloudy Nature of Membership of Modern Entity

Membership of modern entities managing community forests constitutes a source of conflict within local communities. The conditions for adherence to and withdrawal from these entities are determined by the law and Articles of Association of the entities. For instance article 2 (2) of the 1992 law on cooperative societies and CIG is to the effect that:

> No person may be compelled to join or prevented from joining a co-operative society, common initiative group or union of such bodies. Membership within these bodies shall be governed by the provisions of their articles of association....

Article 3 of the 1990 law on freedom of associations stipulates that:

> *Tout membre d'une association peut se retirer à tout moment après paiement des cotisations échues de l'année en cours.*

The above provisions give members the rights to adhere and withdraw from legal entities at will, contrary to what obtains with indigenous institutions where membership is natural and consist of all villagers including minors. For instance adherence into GIC COPAL and DIPAN DI LONG is limited only to those who register. Membership into these legal entities is based upon the payment of an annual registration fee of 5000 FCFA for GIC COPAL,[281] 1000 FCFA annually and 500 FCFA monthly for DIPAN DI LONG. [282]These registration fees are hardly raised by indigenous people and constitute a disincentive for their participation in community forests projects.[283]

The 2008 Simple Management Plan of REPA CIG limits customary user-rights to "all community members for whom the forest has been assigned.... Others (residents) can exercise some of these rights provided they enter into legal contract with the community."[284] It is not clear if this refers to indigenes of the village community or registered members of the modern entity managing the forest? This certainly refers to registered members since the Articles of Association of this entity makes it clear that "membership is void of ethnic background, religious or political affiliation or sex."[285] Such a provision is advantageous to wealthy elites and who meet the registration requirements such as high fees as opposed to indigenous population for which benefit the forest was created, thus defeating the purpose of community forests.

In some regions community forests are single-handedly created by elites who determine those to participate in its management. This is the case of COFAYET community forest. Membership of the legal entity managing this community forest is undefined. The modern entity is said to have been created unilaterally by Mr. Essouma Akono who personally appointed and corrupted some villagers to adhere to it. For instance he is said to have unsuccessfully attempted to bribe Mr. Edjimbi Mba Daniel a native of Ndoundou with the sum of 1.500.000 FCFA should he join his project. He convinced Mr. Voundi Bissa Allexandre a native of Ndoundou and a worker with the National Institute of Cartography permanently resident in Yaounde to proclaim himself as the "Chief of Ndoundou" and appointed as Treasurer Mr. Zolo Edjimbi Samuel. Some of the people he selected to cooperate with were either out of the country or deceased. Examples were Ateba Bitote, Edjibi Ateba, Eyamo Ngo'o and Mbe Assako, all dead before his initiative to create the community forest,

---

281 Article 4 of the Articles of Association of GIC COPAL, 2001.
282 Article 4 of the Articles of Association of DIPAN DI LONG, 2000.
283 Informant: Tim David and Bataké Joseph, notables of Nkokom village 2009.
284 Simple Management Plan, REPA CIG, 2008, p. 42.
285 Article 4 of the Articles of Association of REPA CIG, 2002.

and Reverend Simon Ateba who, within that period was out on a stage in Rome.[286]

The results of this unclear and uncertain membership of modern entities managing community forests serve as a disincentive for the participation of local people. Indigenous people who are marginalised in the creation and management of these forests turn round to oppose the legal entities as was the case of COFAYET. Here villagers of Ndoundou, Olembé, and Meka'a Yetyang over whose territories COFAYET CF spans are in constant conflict with the forest management officer (FMO) who is not a member of the village communities within which territories this community forest is found.[287] In BBNRMC where membership is limited only to indigenes, other residents who do not consider the forest as theirs embarked on destructive exploitation of NTFP which led to conflict with the indigenes.[288] Difficulties in determining who should participate in the management of community forests are clear indications of the choice of wrong partners in the management of community forests in Cameroon. This is because the stakeholders ought to have been well defined before the creation of community forests and not the converse.

Unlike modern entities, membership to indigenous communities is acquired by birth and incorporates all members of the village community. Rational management of community forests will be possible if the management is entrusted to traditional authorities who are considered by the local people as the custodians of the forests and respected by all persons within the community, be they indigenes or strangers.

[286] See confidential letter written by Mr. Ze Bissa Jules, Civil Administrator and heir to the Ndoundou Chieftaincy on 11th May 2001 addressed to the Minister of Environment and Forest requesting the Minister to suspend activities within the COFAYET Bengbis community forest. Equally see letter written to the Minister of Environment and Forest through the S.D.O for Dja et Lobo on 21st of December 1997 by the local communities of Yétyang Ndoundou, Olembé and Meka'a Yétyang requesting the cancellation of Arrêté No. 0001/A/MINEF/DF/SDIF/SA of the 1st of July 1997 creating the COFAYET BENGBIS community forest. This letter was signed by 19 persons among whom were:

- Ateba Thomas, Chief of Ndoundou village;
- Mendoua Meyanga Moise, Chief of Olembé;
- Moneboulou Edjimbi, chief of Meka'a Yetyang.

[287] Ibid.

[288] Interview with Mr. Janvier Mondoa, FMO of BBNRMC, 2009.

4.3.2: Power Struggle between Modern and Indigenous Institutions

Before the advent of the community forests, forests were managed by traditional authorities, in the persons of Fons or Chiefs in collaboration with the forestry administration. Today the management of these forests are placed under legal entities most of which are not headed by traditional authorities who consider these legal entities as having usurped their authorities. The Fon of Kom for instance could not understand why the management of a forest "owned by the Fon" should be given to someone else, and claims that government assistance is misdirected. The Fon and the Traditional Council are fighting to take over the management of the forest from the FMO. This Council sent exploiters to the forest without the consent of the FMO and requested that money derived from this forest be placed under the management of the Fon.[289]

A similar situation was witnessed in GIC JAGRA found in the East Region where there is conflict between the village Chief and the president of GIC JAGRA. There are accusations and counter accusations. While the chiefs accused the GIC for embezzling the community funds, a view upheld by administrative authorities who opened an investigation into the matter,[290] the president of the GIC holds that the chief constitutes an obstacle to the development of the community. He consequently wrote to the administration requesting the replacement of traditional authorities.[291]

Conflict is also rife between legal entities and Village Development Committees (VDC) headed by traditional authorities. The most pronounced was witnessed in Mindourou in the East Region. Here GIC Mindourou manages revenues derived from the exploitation of the community forest, while the VDC manages revenues paid by companies which exploit forests within the village other than the community forests such as PALLISCO a timber exploitation company. The VDC placed under the authority of the Chief has been fighting to take over control and management of the community forest on the basis that since the creation of the community forest GIC Mindourou has not realised any project. On the other hand this legal entity is reluctant to hand over the management of the forest to the VDC on the basis that this committee is headed by the Mayor of Mindourou who will use the proceeds to compensate his political

289 Interview with Mr. Julius Mom Mbzi, FMO of Laikom community forest 2009.
290 Interview with Mr. Nkam Mbuoe Eric D, First Assistant SDO for Haut Nyong 2009.
291 Interview with Chief of Andjouk, 2009.

supporters.[292] This situation of conflicts between traditional institutions and modern entities reached its peak in Zoalabo II community. Here the Chief warned that trees felled will not be useful. Consequently all the trees felled against the wish of the chief were mysteriously cracked.[293]

The above cited conflicts may be attributed to government's choice of wrong partners in the creation and management of community forests. Community forests which ought to enhance sustainable management instead constitute the cause of forest destruction and degradation due to the non respect of SMPs. To solve this problem government should empower local institutions which had from time immemorial managed the forests and are held in very high esteem by the people rather than create parallel institutions which are in constant conflict with traditional institutions and consequently detrimental to the proper and productive management of community forests.

4.3.3: Poor Management: Conflict in the Management Organs of Legal Entities

Difficulties faced in the management of community forests are also due to disagreement between members of executive of legal entities, a situation which is rare in traditional administration. Such conflicts are based on the role of each member of the executive. Even though the Articles of Association of these legal entities clearly spell out the responsibilities of each member, some members the management organs continue to act ultra vires. This is the case with the president of GBOBAPA C.F in the East Region who in addition to his duties as leader of this entity, acts as secretary, financial secretary and treasurer. Other communities such as POKO Zoételé in the South Region and GIC DIPAN DI LONG in the Littoral Region face similar difficulties.[294] In the latter case, the treasure is ignorant of the finances of the community. All documents are in the keeping of the FMO who permanently resides out of the community.[295]

Conflicts between members of executive of legal entities are equally expressed in the constant revision of the bureau of modern entities which is detrimental to the proper management of the forest since the elected

---

292 Interview with Mr. Metoul George, former FMO of GIC Mindourou 2009.
293 Interview with Edourou Vital, Coordinator of PERAD, 2009.
294 Interview with Edourou Vital, Coordinator of PERAD, 2009.
295 Interview with Treasurer of POKO Zoételé, 2009.

officials will not have ample time to implement the SMP. In less than five years the management organ of GIC JAGRA in the East Region had been renewed thrice.[296] If the executives of the management organs of legal entities are unable to develop cordial and friendly working relations, then it becomes doubtful that community forests would be properly manage by potential enemies.

4.3.4: Poor Management: Absence of Entente between Legal Entities and other Stakeholder

The poor relation that exists between government and modern entities is evident in constant conflicts between them. These conflicts are caused by the non respect of the forestry legislations and other commitments as was the case with COFAYET and NDECUDA in the South and South-West Regions respectively. These conflicts led to the suspension of activities in these forests.[297] Since the creation of COFAYET community forest the forest manager has been in constant conflict with both the local community and the administration.[298] The indigenous rulers of these communities requested the suspension of the community forest and the dismissal of the FMO on the bases that he is not the representative of the people.

In Belo the forestry administration collaborates more with indigenous institution rather than the legal entity. Here, culprits arrested from the community forest by the forestry officials were handed to the Fon to be punished in accordance with the rules and customs of the Kom people. The executive of GIC Mindourou is made up of members of the same family. For instance, the FMO, treasurer, financial secretary and the chief are uterine brothers. Villagers therefore consider the community forest as the property of that family and consequently are indifferent concerning its management.[299]

Lack of cooperation between indigenous people and managing organs of the legal entities are mostly based on the fact that local people are not incorporated in community forests management. For instance, the initiator of COFAYET C.F was faced with resistance from local people in the management of this forest due to the fact that the people were not

---

296 Interview with Treasure of GIC JAGRA, 2009.

297 See for instance suspension notification no. 258/04/NSA/MINEF/DPS/DD-DL.

298 See appendix 5.

299 Interview with, Yanga Terence, a native of Mindourou, 2009.

involved in its creation, and consequently knew nothing concerning its management.[300]

The collaborative spirit that rather exists between the traditional institutions and government than between government and legal entities is evident of the fact that wrong partners were chosen for the management of community forests. Consequently the fact that stakeholders involved in the creation and management of community forests can not work in synergy portrays the weaknesses faced in the creation and management of community forests.

4.3.5: Misdirected External Support

Material, financial and technical assistance from government, NGOs and pilot projects to harness the development and management of community forests are misdirected. This view is based on the fact that the beneficiaries of this assistance are foreign rather than indigenous institutions which represent local communities. It was certainly in this light that the Fon of Kom declared that government assistance for the management of forest is misdirected for it is received by the FMO of Laikom community forest and not by traditional authorities who are the custodian of the forests.

The Netherlands Development Organisation (SNV) assists modern entities both financially, materially and technically in the creation and management of community forests. The assistance of this NGO was received by GIC COPAL and GBOPABA. The former manages a community forest in Lékié Division of the Centre Region, while the latter is in charge of a community forest in Lomie Sub-Division of the East Region. The assistance offered by SNV is considered misdirected because these modern entities are not representative of the people and consequently are not accountable to the people for their management. A vivid example of such misdirected assistance was witnessed in Liakom community forest. Here the FMO absconded with money offered by the REGC project and single handedly distributed beehives offered by the same projects to his friends and loved ones,[301] confirming the fact that legal entities are not the right parties to partner with government for the sustainable management of community forest.

[300] Informant, Yanga Terence, a native of Mindourou, 2009.

[301] Interview with, His Royal Highness Yuh Clement, Fon of Kom, 2009.

4.3.6: Wrong Partners in the Creation of Community Forests

Contrary to the provision of 1992 CBD that indigenous communities should be incorporated in the management of forest resources, government approved the creation of legal entities which are not representative of the indigenous communities. Membership to these entities is subject to conditions which local people hardly fulfill. For instance some entities require registration fees which may be as high as 5000 CFAF as is the case of COPAL discussed earlier. These entities are therefore made up of a few individuals who purport to represent local communities when all they care about is their personal interests; and are, consequently not the right partners to sign community forests management agreements with government.

4.4: Indispensable Need for Local Institutions

The State created legal entities from which local communities must make a choice, without taking into consideration the educational levels of the people towards the biophysical, socio-economic and cultural-historical aspects of their environment, which should normally play an important role in the sustainable management of their environment and resources.[302] This implies that all indigenous institutions through which the communities had previously been managing their forests were either considered by the State as incompetent in the management of forest sustainable resources or the State is not truly interested in fostering local management or sustainable management of forest resources.[303] It may be interesting to examine some of the activities of these indigenous institutions in juxtaposition with modern entities in the management of natural resources.

Within local communities, the management of forests and its resources is the responsibility of traditional institution such as the chief and sacred societies. These institutions make rules relating to the management of natural resources and through the traditional council and the Fon instruct the villagers on the utilization of natural resources, especially the forest and other sacred places considered as dwellings for spirits. In

---

[302] Duffield, C., et al., "Local Knowledge in the Assessment of Resource Sustainability: Case studies in Himachal Pradesh, India, and British Columbia, Canada," in Ives, J. D (ed) Mountain Research and Development vol. 18, no. 1, UCP, USA, 1998, p. 36.

[303] Ngwasiri, C. N., "The Community Forestry Programme in Cameroon: A Participatory Management Option? CIFOR, working paper no. 5, Yaounde, 2000, p. 31.

some communities in the South-West Region of Cameroon such as the Bakwerians, it is believed that any exploitation from shrines and forest without the permission of the traditional authorities attracts sanctions inflicted by spirits on the victims. Such a belief is a great deterrent to the commission of the forbidden acts.[304] This is one of the reasons why in African societies, sacrifices are offered and libations poured out not only to appease the spirits but also as signs of gratitude for blessings received. The respect of these local institutions because of the powers they incarnate and the fear of the unknown is more effective than the respect of government institutions and laws whose sanctions are perceptible to the people.

Government on it part collaborates more with traditional institutions than the legal entities created for the management of community forests. For instance, as mentioned earlier, the Fon of Kom, complained that the FMO of Laikom Community forest made away with money collected from the RIGC project. All attempts by *Kwihfon* to bring him to order failed because he claimed not to be answerable to *Kwihfon* for his management. The Fon presented the matter to the SDO for Boyo whose decision was still awaited up to now. Some administrative officials even prefer to use *Kwihfon* rather than State institutions to enforce the respect of forestry legislations. The Chief of Forestry Post of Belo, after tracking down defaulters preferred to hand them to be sanctioned by *Kwihfon* instead of handing them to State Institutions.[305]

There exist no similarities between modern entities and local institutions. Government in order to introduce efficient and viable entities should rather re-enforce existing indigenous institutions. Alternatively the rules should make it mandatory for natives to be part of the entities. This could be done through the traditional councils and Fons or Chiefs, since it is inconceivable that sacred societies such as *Kwihfon* believed never to have been seen, but whose institution functions very effectively in the management of natural resources would become a member of an Association, Economic Interest Group, Corporative Society or Common Initiative Group which alone is now competent to sign management agreements with government on behalf of the local communities.

---

304 Anyangwe, C., The Cameroon Judicial System, Ceper, Yaounde, 1987, p. 14.

305 cf. Funwie, T. C., "Community Forest Management Entities as Effective Tools for Local- Level Participation under Cameroonian Law: Case Study of Kilum/Ijim Mountain Forest." A Thesis Submitted and Publicly Defended in Partial Fulfilment of the Requirement for the Award of a Ph.D in Law, University of Yaounde II, 2007, p. 126.

4.5: Conclusion

Two principal stakeholders are involved in the creation and management of community forests. Government on one the hand represented by MINFOF and local communities on the other represented by legal entities. A critical study of legal entities proves that these entities are not representative of local communities and consequently do not protect their interest. These entities are either out to promote solidarity amongst a specific group of people as is the case with Association or to promote the economic interest of its members as it obtains with CIG. Cooperative and EIG have as principal objective the commercialisation of members' products, distribute profits and ameliorate the economic activities of their members. All these entities were created in the early 90s with the above mentioned objectives which are incompatible with sustainable management of natural resources.

Local institutions made up of chiefs, sacred societies and users group which unfortunately are not qualified to partner with government in the management of community forests are better endowed with the qualities required for sustainable forest management. Chiefs are classified and legally recognised as leaders of the village communities by both government and local communities. They ensure the respect of traditional forest management norms enacted by sacred societies. User-groups (carvers, medicinal plant collectors, bee farmer etc) based on their interest and know-how are specialised in the management of specific NTFP.

The preference given to legal entities rather than indigenous institution in the creation and management of community forests is manifest of the non-incorporation of local communities and consequently the absence of indigenous and customary practices in the management of community forests. If the forest is that of the community as the name implies, then its management should be given the community. Unlike local institutions adherence into legal entities is limited only to a particular class of persons. These entities constantly conflict per se, struggle for power with indigenous institution and lack the cooperation of both indigenous institutions and government. This state of affairs clearly shows the failure of community forests and makes the need to incorporate local institutions in the management of community forest indispensable.

CHAPTER FIVE

TENURE AND THE INTEGRATION OF INDIGENOUS COMMUNITIES IN THE MANAGEMENT OF ENVIRONMENTAL RESOURCES

5.1: Introduction

Land tenure, resource management and use are of great importance in the management of community forests. The development perspectives inherent in sustainable management of community forests require the security of local community's title to land. The application of the Forestry Law is inseparable from land tenure regulation[306] which is a legacy of the Colonial Administration that gives preference to statutory as against customary land tenure which is based on possession from time immemorial and predates colonialism.

The Germans and French Colonial Administrations in Cameroon declared all unoccupied and unexploited lands as *herrenlos* lands and *terre vacante et sans maitre* respectively, meaning vacant lands without masters and placed it under the control of Colonial Administrators, depriving the local community of its ancestral lands and customary ownership. The British recognised customary tenure, but since English law considers forests as constituting an exception to the maxim *quicquid plantatur solo solo cedit*,[307] that is, whatever is attached to land accedes to the land, deprived local communities from claiming rights over such lands.

[306] See section 6 of the Forestry Law which states that "the ownership of forest ... shall be determined by the regulations governing land tenure and State lands and by the provision of this law."

[307] Williams J. in *Lancaster v. Eve* (1859) 141 E.R. 288 at 293.

These colonial policies are adopted by the Cameroonian Legislature which continues to give preference over registered lands. The non-recognition of customary tenure is contrary to the provisions of international instruments[308] has generated more conflicts than harmony between local communities and government, is detrimental to the management of community forests. An example is the Laikom community forest found in Boyo Division of the North West Region, where the local community is in conflict with government over the ownership of forest land. Here while the forestry administration is carrying out reforestation by planting trees, the local community is destroying the trees to cultivate the area. This problem was solved by the introduction of agro-forestry. In Mindourou, a village found in the Haut Nyong Division of the East Region, members of village community claimed ownership of portions of the community forest as belonging to their ancestors.

This chapter portrays the fact that, without secure tenure the participation of local communities in the management of community forests will hardly be a reality. As argued by Chi, communities which own forest rights and secure tenure will have much stronger claims to benefits of potential markets from ecosystem services, and much stronger protection from encroachment than will communities that only have access rights without statutory tenure.[309] Without tenure rights and given the conflicts that this generates, it is doubtful if community forest can be sustainably managed, let alone its existence.

The chapter briefly presents the historical evolution of land and forest tenure, examines the present land and forestry legislation, and how this is addressed by international institutions, such as ILO and UNCHR.

5.2: Background to Land and Forest Tenure

The legal status of land in Cameroon principally deprives local communities from forest ownership is conditioned by concepts introduced in the territory by successive colonial administrations. The Germans were

---

[308] See articles 1 and 27 of the International Convention on Civil and Political Rights; Article 1(4) and 5 of the UN Convention on the Elimination of All Forms of Racial Discrimination; Article 10 of the ILO Convention 169; Article 8 (j) 1992 CBD.

[309] Chi, A. M., " Legal recognition of sacred forests in Cameroon: Giving customary communal ownership rights statutory tenure rights" in Bojang, F. et al., (eds.) Natural Resource Tenure Systems and their Implication for Agriculture, Food Security and Nature Conservation in Africa, Nature and Fauna, vol. 24, Issue 2, FAO, 2010, p. 28.

the first to colonise Cameroon, followed by the French and British.[310] These colonial administrations did shape the country's land and natural resource legislation. The role they played, in determining the legal status of land and forest in Cameroon, favoured statutory as against customary land tenure hence the controversy in ownership of community forests.

It started with the German through an Imperial Decree, the "All-Highest Decree" of 15 June 1896 which declared unoccupied and unexploited lands in the country as *herrenlos* lands, meaning lands without masters. All such lands were vested in the German Crown (*kronland*) apart from lands over which property rights of private individuals, chiefs and native communities were recognised, and lands on which the rights of users had been created by an agreement with the German Colonial Administrators.[311] The effect of this was that all lands not occupied by natives, or over which there was no usage agreement such as fallow lands, hunting grounds, and pastoral lands became crown land. In disregards of the Decree of 15 June 1896, the Germans forced the natives into reserves created by the administration and declared their settlements as "crown land"[312]

As regards the forest, the German enacted two Ordinances dealing with the rights to manage forestry resources. The first, known as the Imperial Forestry Ordinance, was enacted on the 14th of April 1900. This Ordinance empowered the Governor of *Kamerun*[313] to take legislative measures in ensuring that anyone who illegally felled trees for timber replanted the area. The trees could also be replanted by the Governor at the cost of the defaulter.

The second forestry Ordinance enacted by the Germans was in 1913. Paragraph 1 of this Ordinance provided that the exploitation of forest resources from crown land and native reserves could only be done by the Governor or those to whom he had conferred the right.[314] These Ordinances limited the rights of local communities in forest use and

---

[310] This is when the German forces were defeated in the First World War. For more on this, see, Mbuagbaw, T. Y et al., A History of the Cameroon, New Edit, Longman, 1988, p.78.

[311] Tumnde, M. S., "Integrating Law and Local Customs in Forest Resource Management around the Mount Cameroon Region," in Lambi, C. M and Eze, E. B (eds.) A Reading in Geography, UPCA, Bamenda, Cameroon 2001, p. 355.

[312] Ibid.

[313] Cameroon was administered by the Germans from 1884 to 1919. During this period the country was referred to as 'Kamerun'.

[314] cf Tumnde (n 6) 356.

management. Considering that the lands occupied by the natives were essentially made up of farm lands and dwellings, one may conclude that the Germans took control of all forest resources in *Kamerun* and denied the indigenous people ownership and control of their ancestral land and forest.

This deprivation policy which negatively affects the management of community forests today due to lack of secure tenure was equally adopted by the French in a Decree in May 1946. Article 2 of the Decree made it clear that vacant forests as well as fallow lands under regeneration belonged to the State.[315] The implication of this provision just like that of the Germans ordinance was that local communities had no tenure rights over forests and its resources since the only lands which were not vacant and developed were their dwellings and farmlands.

Contrary to the Germans and French policies of assimilation, the British through the 1916 Forestry Ordinance[316] conferred on natives the "customary rights of occupancy" which included rights to use and occupy land. This Ordinance equally recognised the rights of native communities lawfully using and occupying land in accordance with native laws and customs, since these rights were recorded in a special register.[317] This notwithstanding, the appropriation of forest by local communities was not recognised since forest under English law does not constitute part of the land.[318] This implies that, though the British administration recognised the customary rights of local communities over their ancestral land, they did not concede the control and management of forest and its resources by local people. This colonial policy of deprivation contributed in aggravating the forest tenure problems of indigenous communities and influenced current legislation, such as the 1994 Forestry Law. Section 39 (4) of this law even deprives certain NTFP such as ebony, ivory, wild animal horns etc found on private land from ownership by the owner of such land.[319]

5.3: Current Land and Forestry Legislations

After independence in 1960 the Cameroon government undertook to harmonise all past legislation introduced in the country by successive

[315] Ibid p. 358.

[316] See also the Land and Native Rights Ordinance (LNRO) of 1927.

[317] Nzalie, J. E., "Lecture Notes on Land Law," University of Dschang, academic year 2003-2004 (unpublished).

[318] Forest under English law constitute an exception to the maxim *quicquid plantatur solo solo cedit* meaning who ever own the land owns everything on it, up to the sky and everything beneath it.

[319] Article 39 (4) of the 1994 Forestry Law.

colonial masters with those that followed immediately after independence and re-unification in 1972. The outcome of this harmonisation is that land which was effectively occupied by local communities and recognised as such under Germans and French administrations was nationalised as National lands of the first category. Indigenous tenure which was recognised by the British was abolished completely depriving local communities of ownership of land and forest.

The 1974 land legislation which went into force on August 5th 1974 is said to have "abolition" indigenous land rights. This was the interpretation given to Ordinance no. 74/1 of July 6, 1974 by the Minister of Finance at the time. Through a circular letter issued on July 1, 1976 to all Land Consultative Boards in the country, the Minister clearly stated that the 1974 Ordinance *a mis fin a tous les droits fonciers coutumier au Cameroun*, meaning that the Ordinance had put an end to all customary land rights in Cameroon.[320] We hold the opinion that the interpretation given to the Ordinance by the Minister's Circular letter was misleading. In our view the Ordinance did not abolish customary tenure but would simply want them to evolve with time by being registered. It is equally submitted by Ngwasiri that "all unregistered lands in the holding of customary communities or their members continue to be subject to and held under customary law since statutes law can not apply to them so long as they remain unregistered."[321] The case of *Ndefru Zama Odilia, Tumanjong Nanga, & Tawah Mary v. Che Fongwa John*[322] clearly manifest the prevailing influence of customary law in matters of land law.[323]

The preference for registered title greatly weakens the enthusiasm of local communities to participate in management of terrestrial resources. Because they lack proprietary rights over forestland and resources this has negative impact on the management of community forests. This is because communities will not have incentive to manage forests which they are only in possession, but not ownership. This is contrary to international instruments which recommend the recognition of customary land rights.

---

320 Ngwasiri, N. C., The impact of the present land tenure reforms in Cameroon on the former west Cameroon, in Cameroon Law Review, 2rd series Nr 27, CLE, 1984, p. 76.

321 Ibid p. 76.

322 (1998) BCA/3/98 (unreported).

323 Nzalie, J. E., "Dealing in family land and proof of customary law' in Juridis Périodique, no. 51, Yaounde, 2002, p. 35.

5.3.1: Exclusion of Customary Tenure from Statutory Ownership

Land legislation in Cameroon is a legacy of colonial administration. The colonial policy of State ownership of forest land is contained in Cameroon's present land legislation of 1974 which declares that:

> The State shall be the guardian of all lands; it may in this capacity intervene to ensure rational use of land in the imperative interest of the State or economic policies of the nation.[324]

The Ordinance categorises land rights into national lands, State lands and private property. This classification does not recognise communal rights over land and forest is detrimental to the proper management of collective property such as community forests. This acts as a disincentive to the participation of local communities in the management of community forests.

5.3.1.1: Land Tenure Rules Militate Against Community or Customary Ownership

Section 14 of Ordinance no. 74-1 of 6th July 1974 describes national lands as:

> ...lands which at the date when the present ordinance entered into force are not classified into the public or private property of the State and other public bodies.

Section 15 of this Ordinance divides national lands into two categories: to wit:

1) Lands occupied with houses, farms, and plantations and grazing lands manifesting human presence and development;
2) Lands free from any effective occupation.

National lands of the first category comprise lands occupied with houses, farms, and plantations as well as grazing lands manifesting human presence and development. Such lands though not registered are effectively occupied and exploited by local communities. These communities have

[324] Article 2 of Ordinance no. 74-1 of 6th July 1974.

immemorial possession of these lands, as ancestral lands governed by customary tenure.

For instance the Ordinance states in section 17 (2) that:

> ...customary communities members thereof, and any other person of Cameroonian nationality, peacefully occupying or using land in category 1 as defined by article 15, on 5 August 1974, the date of entering into force of the present Ordinance, shall continue to occupy or use the said land. They may apply for land certificate in accordance with the terms of the decree provided for in article 7.

This presupposes that customary communities can register and owned lands, which before 5th August 1974 they were only *de facto* occupants. Does this imply that indigenous communities can own and manage land like collectivities? If so how? Regrettably, the provisions of the law that governs community forests does not provides for such possibilities given that the creation of community forest is by virtue of a management agreement between government and local community concerned. The law does not specify the possibility of the community owning the forest in the long term, let alone when the agreement comes to an end. This can be inferred from the 1994 Forestry Law which provides that:

> The services in charge of forests shall in order to promote the management of forest resources by village communities which so desire, give them assistance. An agreement shall then be signed between the two parties...[325]

It is argued that occupation or possession is proof of ownership. Occupation refers to the act of occupying a property which has no ownership[326] while possession is the control which someone has over property.[327] Possession entails the right to the occupation and enjoyment of property. It is subordinate to ownership which includes the rights of

325 Sections 37 (1) of the 1994 Forestry Law.

326 Collins, P., Dictionary of law, PCP, Great Britain, 2000, p. 250.

327 Ibid p. 279.

alienation and destruction.[328] Possession by local community is evidence of ownership as was held in the American case of *Mayagna (Sumo) Awas Tingni Community v. The State of Nicaragua* that:

The customary law of indigenous people should specially be taken into account because of the effect that flows from it. As a product of customary law, possession of land should suffice to entitle indigenous communities without title to their land to obtain official recognition and registration of their rights to ownership.[329]

In this case the State of Nicaragua was held liable for violating the rights to property embodied in article 21 of the American Convention on Human Rights and the American Declaration on the Rights and Duties of Man, by granting a concession to a company to carry out road construction and logging on the Awas Tingni lands without the consent of the community.

In granting judgment in favour of the Awas Tingni community, the Inter-American Court of Human Rights observed that:

> ...by their very existence indigenous community have the right freely on their own territories; the close relationship that communities have with the land must be recognised and understood as a foundation for their cultures, spiritual life, and cultural integrity and economic survival. For indigenous communities the relationship with the land is not merely one of possession and production, but also a material and spiritual element that they should fully enjoy, as well as a means through which to preserve their cultural heritage and pass it on to future generations.

The court held among others that:

> The State must adopt measures of a legislative, administrative and other character necessary

[328] Nzalie, J. E., "Does the Doctrine of Adverse Possession Constitutes an infringement on the Fundamental Human Right to the owner of Property?" A.F.S.J.P, University of Dschang, 2002. p. 181.

[329] Colchester, M. et al., A Survey of Indigenous Land Tenure, FAO, FPP, UK, 2001, p. 13.

> to create an effective mechanism for official delimitation, demarcation and titling of indigenous community property in accordance with the customary law, value, usage and customs of these communities.

This case affirms the validity of indigenous form of communal property and the fact that indigenous territorial rights arise by virtue of traditional occupation and use and indigenous form of tenure rather than from grants, recognition or registration by the State.

The right of possession by local communities is expressed in the fact that they control the use of their land and prevent intruders. Such intention may be inferred from any development on the land, however minute. This was the opinion held by Ekema, J., in *Ndange v. Ngeh*[330] in the following words:

> If a man owns a large piece of land and develops part of it, no matter small the area developed is, he is in possession of the whole of that land, if not actually at least constructively. Even if no development has been carried out on that land over which he has title he has at least constructive possession and he can expel any intruder.[331]

The Canadian Supreme Court in *Calder v. Attorny General of British Columbia*[332] held that possession is of itself proof of ownership, which includes the power of disposal. A similar decision was arrived at by Lamer, C. J., in *Delgamuukw v. British Columbia.*[333] Here the judge held that possession is based on pre-sovereign occupation and indigenous customs and practices. Following the same trend of reasoning the Australian High Court in *Wik Peoples v. Queensland & Ors*[334] declares that indigenous land rights arise from operation of the law and does not depend on any grant from the crown (government). In passing his judgment, Brennan C. J.,

330 (1975) BCA/16/74 (unreported).

331 See also the dictum of Privy Council in Wuta-Ofei v. Danguah (1961) 1 WLR 1238 at 1243, cf. Nzalie, J.E., "Dealing in family land and proof of customary law' in Juridis Périodique, no. 51, Yaounde, 2002, p. 36.

332 [1973] 34 DLR (3d) 145, at 190.

333 [1997] 3 S.C.R, 1010, 1082.

334 [1997] 187 CLR 1, at 84

stated unequivocally that "native title does not require any conduct on the part of any person to complete it, nor does it depend for its existence on any legislative, executive or judicial declaration. But in Cameroon natives are required to have their rights registered.

Land ownership in Cameroon is by statutory titles obtained through a registration process on national lands of the first category. Community forests can't be created from this category of lands which implies that local communities cannot claim ownership of forest located on this category of land.

National lands of the second category from which community forests can be created are described as lands free from effective occupation or exploitation.[335] The above description is misleading because it invariably includes land held by local communities such as indigenous forestlands. More so, there is no land free from effective occupation or exploitation. The land contemplated by this provision of the law were exploited since time immemorial by local communities for hunting, grazing, spiritual practices or even as dwelling as is the case with Petit Pol pygmy community in the East Region.

Confirming the immemorial exploitation of land by local communities the 1995 Forestry Decree stipulates that:

> Forest which may be subject to community management shall be those situated on the outskirt or close to one or more communities and in which the inhabitants carry out their activities.

The creation of community forest from this category of lands could be interpreted as government's acknowledgement of the immemorial possession of these lands by local communities which ought to be evidence of ownership as was the situation in the *Awas Tingi* case discussed earlier. Unfortunately lands of the second category cannot the subject of ownership by local communities. Such lands and their resources have been appropriated by the State which apparently manages it with local communities.

State ownership of forest is not limited to Cameroon. It is equally true of other countries of the Congo Basin such as Gabon and DRC. In DRC

[335] See article 15 (2) of Ordinance no. 74-1 of 6th July 1974 to establish rules governing land tenure.

for instance article 7 of the 2005 Forestry Code asserts State ownership over all areas of forest.[336] Elsewhere in the world such as in Guyana and Malaysia the State equally owns virtually all forests. In Guyana, about 13.6 million of the 16.9 million hectares of forest in that country have been classified as State forest, while in Malaysia, except for a few thousands hectares of privately owned plantation forests, all forests are owned by the Federated State.[337]

In Guatemala, following a 1996 Peace Agreement, communities could apply for and manage forest concessions for 25 year renewable, but the State remains as landowner.[338] Under the 1997 Land Law of Mozambique, the State remains the owner of land and may transfer permanent use and benefits rights to communities. The community may register such rights in the national cadastre and a formal certificate is issued to the community. In Nepal land remains officially property of the State which gives communities control of forest resources. About 25% of Nepal´s forest land is managed by over 14.000 community Forest User Groups (CFUGs).[339] In Brazil the ownership of all land rests with the State and each of the categories of forest land takes that as a starting point, transferring some level of control, management and access to benefits to the communities. Indigenous rights have formally been recognised in the Brazilian constitution and government is demarcating and formally recognising indigenous territories through presidential decrees.[340] Some 12% of Brazil national land territory is currently designated as indigenous land paving way for the recognition of customarily owned lands.

Conversely in some countries, portions of natural forest could be owned by individual or communities. For instance, in Papua New Guinea, (PNG) ownership of forest resources is vested with the customary owner of the land. In this country, 97% of land is held under customary law and 3% by the State and private entities. Here commercial forestry operation cannot take place on customary land unless the government has acquired forest management rights from the customary land owner.[341]

---

[336] Cotula, L. et al., Tenure in REDD, Start-point or afterthought? IIED, UK, 2009, p. 35.
[337] Ibid p. 45.
[338] Long, C., Forest and Community control: Official process that permits formal recognition of community management and rights and their relevance to the Democratic Republic of Congo, IIED, 2010, p. 8.
[339] Ibid p. 10.
[340] Ibid p. 6.
[341] Ibid p. 49.

The Uganda constitution, vests ownership of land in citizens rather than the State and under the 1998 Land Act customary tenure is given same recognition as any other tenure.[342] In this country 70% of the forests are in private and community hands while 30% are in forest reserves and national parks.[343] In Tanzania 70% of land is considered as village land, owned by communities. Villages are recognised as landowners and decisions concerning land and forest management are taken at village council level. In Scotland, community forests are owned and managed by local communities with the right to buy or lease land.[344] In the US case of *United State v. Shoshone tribe of Indians*[345] local communities´ title was defined to include mineral rights, rights to commercially exploit timber, fish and game and water rights. A similar definition was adopted in the Canadian case of *Delgamuukw* where Lamer, C. J stated that aboriginal title encompass mineral rights. Such a policy increases the zeal of local communities to participate in the sustainable management of natural resources.

The outcome is that local communities only enjoy usufructuary rights and not ownership giving rise to conflicts in the management of community forests which conflicts cannot guarantee sustainability of the forest. A vivid example is the case of the Laikom community forest in the North-West Region. Here the local people and the forestry administration could not come to a compromise on the use of some portions of the forest. While the local people preferred to farm this portion on the grounds that it is their ancestral farmland, that it belonged to their ancestors, the Forestry Officials prioritised trees planting on the basis that the land belonged to the State. This led to open confrontations between the administration and the local community over the determination of the proprietorship of the forestland. Similar difficulties were faced in the creation of "Boomaboong and Pouth-Njock" (BOPO) community forest found in the Littoral Region. Here some members of the community were reluctant to consider some portions of the forest as constituting part of the community forest. To them these portions were owned by their ancestors and consequently belong to their families.[346]

---

[342] Ibid p. 13.

[343] Ibid p. 14.

[344] Ibid.

[345] 304 US 111 (1938) cf. Colchester, M. et al., A Survey of Indigenous Land Tenure, FAO, FPP, UK, 2001, p. 17.

[346] Interview with Ntamack Philibert, the Secretary of BOPO community, (Pouth-Ndjock 7 April 2009).

As regards collective ownership, it is reported that 7% of the world's forest is owned by local communities.[347] Most States are legally recognising the rights of local communities to own and mange forest resources such as Indonesia, Mauritania, Botswana and Papua New Guinea. In Indonesia for instance the 1999 Forestry Law recognises the existence of customary communities and provides that their forestlands should be demarcated and officially recognized.[348] In Mauritania, the *Code Pastoral* enacted in 2000 and published in 2004 embodies a combination of both traditional and Shari'a law and codifies the customary tenure of pastoralists. In this country, collective or private interests on land cannot be established without the permission of customary land users. In Botswana the Tribal Land Act of 1968 prioritised the use of indigenous tenure in the administration of land.[349] These policies recognise indigenous as opposed to statutory tenure. If similar policies are adopted for Cameroon, they will certainly serve as an incentive for the effective participation of indigenous communities in the management of community forests.

State sovereignty is vested over lands belonging to private persons, and lands which can actually be described as State lands, in the sense that the State has ownership of them and can do with them as it pleases. Such lands are classified into two categories, to wit, the public property of the State and the private property of the State leaving no opportunity for community ownership. The public property of the State is composed of:

> All personal and real property which, by their nature or intended purpose is set apart either for the direct use of the public, or for the public service.[350]

Such property "shall be inalienable, imprescriptible and unattachable..."[351] By inalienable it implies that the public property of the State cannot be disposed of either permanently or temporarily. Imprescriptible implies that there is no specific time or duration within which such property is expected to exist. It must endure forever. Un-attachable signifies that no person can attach public property for the

347 Cotula (n 31) 12.
348 Cotula (n 31) 42.
349 Knox, A. et al., "Integrating customary land tenure into statutory land law" available at www.usaid.gov (consulted 12/03/2011).
350 Article 2 (1) of Ordinance no. 74/2 of 6 July 1974 to establish rule governing State lands.
351 Ibid article 2 (2).

payment of his debts, not even the President of the Republic.[352] The above characteristics clearly show that local communities would under no circumstances claim ownership of any portion the public property of the State. Although some categories of forests protected areas may be classified under State lands, community forests are not designed from State lands but from national lands of the second category.

The State has the prerogative to dispose of its private property. This may be:

- Allocated to public services;
- Assigned to public bodies;
- Alloted as a contribution to the capital of companies with a right or reincorporation in the private property of the State in the event of dissolution, bankruptcy, or liquidation of the said company;
- Alloted leasehold or freehold to natural persons or corporate bodies;
- Alloted leasehold or freehold to international bodies of which Cameroon is a member;
- Alloted leasehold or freehold and subject to reciprocity to diplomatic or consular missions accredited to Cameroon.[353]

It is clear from the above provision that the State has the prerogative to dispose of its private property including landed property by allotment, allocation or assignment. These are administrative act of giving out or distributing property. While an allotment confers the right of ownership, an allocation only confers a right of possession[354] and an assignment refers to the legal transfer of a property or a right.[355]

The private property of the State can only be disposed of, for the benefits of public services, public bodies, companies, natural persons or corporate bodies, international bodies, diplomatic or consular missions and not indigenous communities. Since indigenous communities are short of corporate personality they cannot benefit from the disposal of the private property of the State. Village communities in Cameroon composed of collectivities therefore cannot own and manage community forests like corporate bodies, which are organisations recognised by law.

---

352 Nzalie (n12).
353 Article 12 of Ordinance no. 74/2 of 6 July 1974 to establish rule governing State lands.
354 Nzalie (n12).
355 Collins (n 21) 25.

5.3.1.2: Private Forests

The Forestry Law classifies private forests as:

> Forests planted" by natural persons or corporate bodies on land they acquired in accordance with the laws and regulations in force. Owners of such forests shall draw up a management plan with the assistance of the services in charge of forests, in order to ensure sustained and durable yield.[356]

Planted forests are man-made forests which must be distinguished from natural forest. The classification of private forest proffered here excludes the possibility of local communities owning "natural forests." Even where land and forest are owned by individuals or corporate bodies, the forestry law prohibits the ownership of some forest products such as:

> Ebony, ivory, wild animal horns as well as certain animals and plants and medicinal species or those which are of particular interest...[357] found in "natural forests" on lands belonging to private individuals, shall be the property of the State except where the said products have been acquired by the person concerned in accordance with the laws and regulations in force.[358]

Does this imply that an individual can have title on "natural forest" in Cameroon? If so how can this be done, given that this obtains in other countries as earlier discussed.

To re-enforce its control over forests on private lands, limiting the rights of the landowners to use or dispose of their lands as they please, the forestry law requires that:

> The initiation of any development project that is likely to perturb a forest or aquatic environment

---

356 Section 39 (1&2) of the 1994 Forestry Law.
357 Ibid section 9 (2).
358 Ibid section 39 (4).

> shall be subject to a prior study of environmental hazard.[359]

The owners of forestlands nevertheless have a right of pre-emption in the event of sale of any natural products found in "their forests."[360] This implies that even though individuals are free to plant trees on land owned by them, they are not free to make use of the trees as they desire, attributable to the ecosystem functions of the forests.

Private forest does not exist since customary laws which govern the lives of local communities' favours communal as against individual ownership of land. This may certainly be one of the reasons why more than two decades ago since the introduction of the registration system giving local communities the opportunity to have their lands registered, only about 6% of rural lands have been registered.[361] It is alleged that this is due to the registration process which is administratively long, sophisticated, cumbersome, costly and time consuming. An attempt by the President of the Republic to simplify the procedure did not yield much fruits. The Presidential Decree issued to this effect neither took into account rural specificity nor addressed the question of the actual status of indigenous land tenure which constitute the real problem of rural communities.[362] We therefore share Funwie opinion that if the Decree has made any inroads in the process of registration, it is only for the urban population because the difficulties inherent in the 1976 Decree have not been removed.[363]

As opposed to private forests derived from national lands of the first category which are generally planted by individuals, community forests are natural forest estate created from lands of the second category which the State concedes to local communities not to own but to manage in partnership with government. Even if a local community acquires title on a piece of forestland as could be deduced from the provision of article 9 (a) of Decree no 76-165 of 27 April 1976, the forests cannot constitute community forests. This is because community forests are classified from

---

359 Ibid section 39 (2) and 16 (3).

360 Ibid section 9 (5).

361 Farcacque, G and Mc Auslan, P., Reforming Urban Land Policies and Institutions in Developing Countries, The World Bank Washington, D.C 1992, p. v.

362 Decree no. 2005/481 of 16 December 2005 modifying and completing certain provisions of Decree no. 76/165 of 27th April 1976 to establish the conditions for obtaining land certificates.

363 cf. Funwie, T. C., "Community Forest Management Entities as Effective Tools for Local- Level Participation under Cameroonian Law: Case Study of Kilum/Ijim Mountain Forest." A Ph.D Thesis, University of Yaounde II, 2007.

lands of the second category which are not subject to private ownership. In order to encourage the active participation of local communities in forests management, their customary or communal ownership of realty (i.e. landed property), that existed from time immemorial in the management of their environment should be legally recognised. This is the case in countries such as Bolivia, New Zealand and Nepal outside the African continent as well as Ghana, Botswana, South African, Uganda, Niger, Namibia, and Tanzania within Africa have enacted law legally recognising customary tenure.[364] Since 1974, Peru had specific legislations that recognised indigenous communities' title to land and the State has signed ILO Convention 169 on the rights of indigenous and tribal people that will be discussed later. In Gambia ownership of land is vested in customary institutions rather than the State. Here in order to manage a community forest the community must present an attestation from the traditional chief that it has customary ownership rights to the land or that permission has been given by the customary owners to annex the land for community use.[365] In South Africa for instance, all legislation restricting black land ownership and use were repealed, such as the Natives Land Act, legislation passed in 1913.[366] Today the Khomani San of South Africa have gained secure access to a large proportion of the Kgalagadi Park where they practice their culture.[367]

5.3.2 Abolition of Concept of Community Land and Forest

Before 6th July 1974, land holding in Cameroon could be classified under a number of headings, including land holding by the community and land holding by the family at the level of the local community. This came about as a result of the fact that land was initially acquired by the collective effort of the entire village either peacefully or through war. The land became the common property of the entire village community. To quote Kamga:

> *La terre est le principal bien collectif dans le droit coutumier. Les terres du village oeuvre de conquête de tout les habitants est non d'une personne,*

---

[364] Knight, R., "The Community Land Titling Initiative: An Investigation into the Protection of Customary Land claims" in Erica Harper, (ed.) Working with Customary Justice Systems: Post-Conflicts and Fragile States, IDLO, 2011, p. 145.

[365] Long (n 33) 12.

[366] O'Meara, Patrick, and Winchester, N. Brian., "Natives Land Act." Microsoft® Student, Encarta, 2009.

[367] Colchester, M. et al., A Survey of Indigenous Land Tenure, FAO, FPP, UK, 2001, p. 53.

> *représentaient un bien collectif, un bien commun, à l'acquisition duquel tout le monde a collaboré. La propriété privée foncière n'existe pas à l'origine dans le droit coutumier.*[368]

The idea here is that when a group settled, members appropriated parcels of land on behalf of their families. The parcels not identifiable to any family constituted community land, and were set aside for communal use. This category of land included forestland, market sites, graveyards, shrines, ceremonial grounds, chieftaincy and lands attached to it. Chieftaincy land is regarded as community land since such land passes to the successor of the chief and not to his descendants. Successor here refers to one who takes over from the deceased while descendant include the general heir of the deceased.

Community land and forest was held by the chief for the interest of, and managed on behalf of the local community through their deputies like traditional councils, quarter heads and lineage heads.[369] Therefore Ownership of unoccupied parcels of land remains vested in the village community as a whole and not in the chief and his family. Judicially Cameroonian chiefs, have no claim to ownership of village land as could be found in a Bamenda court of appeal case between *Presbyterian Church Moderator v. D.C Johnny.*[370] In this case the court dismissed the assertion of the chief of Mankon that all land in Mankon belongs to him. The court made it clear that the chief holds the Mankon land not in his name but in the name of the people of Mankon. Chiefs enjoy only administrative rights of supervisory oversight of village land for the benefit of the whole community.[371]

As stated by Gwanmesia, J., in *Chief Lobe Njembele v. Benedict Nsombai*[372]:

> ...The chief is a mere trustee holding lands for the common benefit of the natives. Chiefs are in no way land owners of the communal lands over

[368] cf. Anyangwe, C., "Land Tenure and Interests in Land", in Cameroon Law Review, 2nd series Nr 27, 1984, p. 33.

[369] Nkwi, W. G., "Boundary conflicts in Africa: A case study of Bambili and Babanki-Tungoh (North West Province of Cameroon), C. 1950-1995)", in Journal of Applied Social Sciences, Vol. 6, no. 1&2, University of Buea, Cameroon, 2007, p. 19.

[370] (1974) BCA/27/74 (unreported).

[371] Elias, T. O., The nature of African customary law, Manchester University Press, 1956, p. 164.

[372] (1980) CASWP/20/70 (unreported).

> which they are chiefs unless a piece of land belongs
> to him in his personal capacity.

A similar ruling had been delivered in 1967 in the case of *Chief Thompson Ewone v. Attorney-General and Director of land and Survey.*[373] In this case the West Cameroon Federal Court of Justice held that according to the Bakweri native laws and customs, native land is communal land to which no individual in the community has a title and no individual, be he a chief or not, can make a disposition without the consent of the community.

As described by Speed, C. L., in *Amodu Tijani v. Secretary Southern Nigeria*[374] the chief's right over land is in the nature of a "seigneurial right giving him right of control and management of the land, in accordance with the well-known principles of native law and custom."[375] But neither the chiefs nor any individual could dispose of the community land.

Since the enactment of Ordinance no. 74/1 of 6th July 1974, governing land tenure in Cameroon, land holding by the local community no longer forms one of the categories of land tenure in Cameroon. This Ordinance apparently abolished all land rights held under customary law. Lands which initially fell into the category of community lands from which community forests ought to be found are today owned and managed by the State either as national lands or as State lands.

The *de facto* existence of customary tenure is not unique to Cameroon. This method of land holding characterised by communal ownership and the inalienability of land remains the predominant method of land holding in Africa. To indigenous people it even remains the dominant system used to assert their rights to land including the forest. Colchester cites Niger as one of the best documented cases. In this country, though government took a stand against customary system by limiting the powers of the chiefs to allocate lands in their areas, customary tenure continue to operate *de facto*. To become *de jure*, the government by 1970 began integrating formal and customary systems into one legal framework called "Code Rurale" within which there is a strong impulsion

373 cf. Anyangwe (n 63) 37.
374 [1921] 2 AC 399.
375 cf. Anyangwe (n 63) 37.

for titling.[376] Even though titling directly contradicts indigenous tenure, and government is mistrusted, customary rules continue to apply[377] or co-exist with modern law.

This strong reliance on customary tenure by local communities contrasted by statutory tenure by government constitutes one of setbacks in the sustainable management of community forests. As rightly observed by Murphree:

> Communities can become effective institutions for sustainable resource management, only if they are granted genuine proprietorship, that is the right to use resources, determine the mode of their usage, benefit fully from their use, determine the distribution of such benefits and determine rules of access. Any policy which excludes these components will frustrate the goal of making communities effective institutions for resource management.[378]

5.3.3 Disrespect of Customary Tenure

In Cameroon, more than 250 customary laws[379] co-exist with statutory laws, certain basic uniform principles have evolved in the domain of customary tenure, notably the principle of inalienability and communal ownership of land.[380] The application of these customary law principles is guaranteed by national and international instruments and jurisprudence.[381]

Nationally the Constitution[382] attribute customary rights to the local people and at the same time limits its application, rendering it a precarious right. For instance it is provided in the preamble of the Constitution that

---

376 Colchester (n 62) 59.

377 cf. Colchester (n 62) 59.

378 Murphree, M. W., "Communities as resource management institutions," Gatekeepers series, no. 36, IIED, 1993.

379 Ngwafor, E. N., Family law in Anglophone Cameroon, University of Regina Press, Saskatchewan, Canada, 1993, p.1; See also Gaillard, P., Le Cameroun Tome 1 Editions L'Harmttan, Paris, 1989, p. 13, where this author rather talks of 207 tribes and consequently 207 customs.

380 *Chritopher v. Anye Henry Saningong* Appeal no. BCA/7cc/92 (unreported).

381 *Eshugbayi V. Nigerian Government (1931) AC 662, Enjema Liote V. Hannah Forty [1948]. CASWP/CC/15/82 Alexander Duru V. Haddison Masalo,[1948]CASWP/CC/52/80.*

382 Preamble of the 1996 Cameroon Constitution rendered enforceable by article 65.

"the State shall ensure the protection of minorities and preserve the rights of indigenous population in accordance with the law."

The above requirement entails the preservation of the rights of local communities including rights to manage and develop their ancestral lands and forests. The constitution affirms Cameroon's attachment to all duly ratified conventions[383] and most of the conventions discussed provide for the protection of traditional values. The recognition and protection of the rights to property and traditional values indirectly extends to the recognition of traditional land tenure system composed of communal ownership of land. Qualifying phrases such as "in accordance with the law" used in the preamble of the constitution will weaken the projected constitutional guarantee and provide legal opportunities for government to overrides these provisions through administrative processes.[384] For instance the 1994 Forestry Law does not provide for ownership by local communities of natural forest, nor the 1996 Law on Environmental Management. The latter only calls on the population to participate in environmental management in the following words:

> The population shall be encouraged to participate in environmental management through... representation of populations within environmental advisory bodies...production of environmental information, sensitisation, training, research and education on the environment.[385]

The Southern Cameroons High Court Law 1955[386] provides for the enforcement and observance of every native law and custom which is not repugnant to natural justice, equity and good conscience. The above cited native law and custom certainly include customary tenure which has been the main form of land holding by local communities.

The non-recognition of customary tenure over forest resources has rather created conflicts than mutual and participatory management.

---

383 Part VI of the 1996 Cameroon Constitution.

384 Nchunu, S., "Managing Land Use and Environmental Conflicts in Cameroon" A Paper presented at the second colloquium of the IUCN Academy of Environmental Law on Environmental Law and Land Use, 4th to 8th October 2004, University of Nairobi.

385 Section 72 of the 1996 Environmental Law.

386 See section 27 (1) S.C.H.C.L 1955.

An example by Nchunu[387] is the community forest project in Kilum mountain region which met with a lot of resistance from Oku graziers with the support of their traditional leader. This resistance degenerated into conflicts between the local community and the Staff of the Kilum/Ijim Forest Project igniting a series of court actions.[388] *In the People of Cameroon V. Isaiah Mangeh & 138 Ors,*[389] the Bamenda court of appeal ordered Oku graziers to demolish all the huts and fences which they had constructed within the confines of the Kilum mountain forest which is a State reserve. Despite the court decisions against the indigenous people of Oku, they have continued to graze in their ancestral land frustrating the community forest initiative in the area. The late Fon of Oku is even quoted as saying that "the day goats will be taken away from the hills of the Kilum mountain, he too will also be taken away from Oku."[390] Conflicts of ownership equally led to open confrontations within the Laikom community between the local community and the forestry administration in the course of which the tools of the local people were ceased by the forestry administration.

Internationally the 1992 CBD, equally call on member States, to:

> ...respect, preserve and maintain knowledge, innovations and practices of indigenous and local communities embodying traditional lifestyles relevant for the conservation and sustainable use of biological diversity...[391]

Similar provision could equally be found in International Human Rights Instruments such as 1986 African Charter on Human and Peoples' Rights, 1976 International Convention on Civil and Political Rights, 1976 International Covenant on Economic, Social and Cultural Rights, 1989 UN Convention on the Rights of the Child, 1969 UN Convention on the Elimination of All Form of Racial Discrimination, 2007 UN Declaration on the Rights of Indigenous People and the International Labour Organisation (ILO) Convention 169 which will be examined later.

---

387 Nchunu (n 79) 10.

388 *Amidou Lukong V. Razel Road Construction Company Ltd. HCK/5/95* (unreported). *Kimbi Moses Ndoh V. Groupement D'Entreprise Trapp-Strabag Belfinger + Berger*, WHC/2/98 (unreported).

389 BCA/35/2002 delivered on 16 July 2003 (unreported).

390 *The People V. Isaiah Mangeh & 138 Ors* (2003) (unreported), BCA/35/2002 delivered on 16 July 2003 p. 3.

391 Article 8 (j) 1992 CBD.

The creation of community forests gives the impression that the community has the requisite potentials in the management of forest, such as existing indigenous knowledge and cultural practices as provided for by article 8 (j) of the 1992 CBD. This could be mitigating or legitimate reasons for recognising their customary rights and eventual ownership of such forests. By subjecting community forests to the authority of MINFOF with powers to annul the management agreement unilaterally, confirms the fact there are no prospects of a community ever owning such a forest in future, let alone their sustainable management.

The non-recognition of indigenous ownership of forestlands constitutes one of the fundamental causes of forest crises in Asia. When government nationalised all woodlands in Napel in 1957, it let to rapid forest degradation which compelled the government to transfer back the woodlands to local communities.[392] In Sweden where community forest has been practised for more than a century, the community forest known as "forest common" which is effectively owned by the community has survived since 1862.[393]

The recognition of community ownership of forest land is important not only for the tangible benefits, the ecosystem services and cultural values of the forest, but equally in determining eligibility for incentives, within the context of the United Nations collaborative programme on Reducing Emission from Deforestation and forest Degradation (REDD) in developing countries. One of the advantages of REDD is to compensate for the protection of forest. If the ownership of the forest is not clarified, this compensation may be misdirected. The question is will the compensation be given to government who is the owner of the forest, or to local communities which actually manage the forest? This difficulty can only be solved if tenure rights of the forest are clearly defined.

Tenure rights will be ascertained by the acquisition of a land certificate which constitutes the official certification of real property rights.[394] This implies that secured ownership will guarantee the official recognition of the community's title defined as including mineral rights.[395]

---

[392] Nchunu, S., "Land tenure system and community forests management in Cameroon" (unpublished).

[393] Ibid.

[394] Article 1 (1) of Decree no. 76/165 of 17 April 1976 to establish the conditions for obtaining land certificates amended and supplemented by Decree no. 2005-481 of 16 December 2005.

[395] See *United State v. Shoshone tribe of Indians* 304 US 111 (1938).

Local communities holding land under customary law are therefore considered as occupiers unless such interests are registered.

Registration serves as security of title, based on the insurance principle which is to the effect that registered title is protected against adverse claims. Registration is said to insure the land against all interests that are not registered such as minor interests and cannot be qualified as overriding interests. Minor interest are defined by section 52 (1) of the Registration of Title Act cap 181, of the 1935 laws of Nigeria as "all rights and interests which are not registered or protected on the register and are not overriding interests." Overriding interests on the other hand are defined by section 3 (xvi) of the 1925 English Land Registration Act as "all encumbrances, interest, rights and power not entered on the register but subject to which registered disposition are by this Act, to take effect. These interests are considered as "those interests which by their nature are so conspicuous that any prudent person interested in a piece of land ought to be aware of, and for that reason do not need to be entered in the register to be protected by law."[396]

Land registration facilitates conveyance, based on the mirror and curtain principles. This is because before a title is registered it must have been thoroughly investigated and found to be unimpeachable.[397] As a mirror, the land register is said to reflect accurately and completely and beyond all arguments, the current facts that are material to a man's title. As a curtain, registration protects the title from unregistered titles.[398]

Land registration gives a title which can serve as collateral security especially with the coming into force of the Treaty for the Harmonisation of Business Law in Africa commonly known by its French acronym as OHADA[399] and the recently created Farmer's Bank. This bank gives the opportunity for farmers including those involve in the forestry sectors to raise loans needed for the sustainable management of forest resources. Through the OHADA Treaty a good number of Uniform Acts (UA) have been enacted among which is the Uniform Act on Securities which emphasises on security or collateral as guarantees for loans.[400]

---

[396] Nzalie (n 23) 185.

[397] Egute, M. A., Essentials of Nigerian Land LAW, OPPC, Nigeria, 2002, p. 246.

[398] cf. Nzalie, J. B., « The law on the registration of instruments under common law and civil law jurisdictions: the case of Cameroon" in Juridis Périodique no. 48, 2001, p. 75.

[399] Organisation pour L'"Harmonisation du Droit des Affaires en Afrique.

[400] Article 119 of UA on Securities.

Unfortunately, though the local communities "own" numerous hectares of land, they cannot use these lands as security for loans due to the fact that they lack title over the said lands depriving community forests of such financial opportunities, for banks are less likely to lend to those in physical possession of land but with no formal recognised rights to the land.[401] All the pieces of legislation dealing with forest resources exert an influence in favour of the country's statutory tenure and subject the ownership of forest to land tenure.[402]

5.4: International Recognition of Indigenous Tenure

Notwithstanding that the current land legislation in Cameroon and other countries of the Congo Basin continue to deprive local communities of customary tenure rights, the recognition of indigenous land right is rather expanding. This is evidenced in International Human Rights Instruments such as the International Labour Organisation (ILO) Convention 169 which will be examined seriatim.

5.4.1: Human Rights Instruments

International Human Rights Instruments recognise and enforce the rights of indigenous people to own and use land and resources which they traditionally occupy. An example is the 1986 African Charter on Human and Peoples' Rights. Article 14 of this charter guarantees the right to property and stipulates that it "may only be encroached upon in the interest of public need or in the general interest of the community and in accordance with the provisions of appropriate laws."

Article 1 of the 1976 International Convention on Civil and Political Rights (ICCPR) acknowledges local peoples' rights to self- determination in the following words:

> All people have the right of self-determination. By virtue of that right they freely determine their political status and freely pursue their economic, social and cultural development.

[401] Knight, R., "The Community Land Titling Initiative: An Investigation into the Protection of Customary Land claims" in Erica Harper, (ed.) *Working with Customary Justice Systems: Post-Conflicts and Fragile States*, IDLO, 2011, p. 146,

[402] See section 6 of the 1994 Forestry Law.

This right is defined amongst others by the International Covenant on Economic, Social and Cultural Rights (ICESCR) as the rights of the people to freely dispose of their natural wealth and resources. These people may equally not be deprived of their own means of subsistence.[403] The Human Right Commission (HRC) in it concluding observation on the reports of Mexico and Norway in 1999 and that of Australia in 2000 maintained that States should implement and respect the rights of indigenous people to self-determination, particularly in respect of their traditional lands.[404]

Article 27 of the 1976 ICCPR provides:

> In those States in which ethnic, religious or linguistic minorities exist, persons belonging to such minorities shall not be denied the right, in community with other members of their group, to enjoy their own culture, to profess or practice their own religion, or to use their own language.

Elaborating on article 27 in 2000, the HRC stated that article 27 requires that necessary steps be taken to restore and protect the title of indigenous persons in their native lands. The protection of religious and cultural sites of local people is contemplated. The practise of community forests in Cameroon is not compatible with the above provisions as customary tenure is not recognised and rights to use forest resources for subsistence may even be suspended.[405] The choice of foreign partners in the management of community forests discussed in chapter four is a clear indication that local communities are deprived of the ownership and use of community forest for their cultural practices.

The 1989 UN Convention on the Rights of the Child equally recognises the rights of indigenous communities to own and manage their ancestral lands. Article 30 of this Convention protects cultural rights in case of indigenous children and by implication indigenous people as a whole. Contrary to article 30, youths are hardly incorporated in the management of community forest. This is evidence in the absence of young people in Nkokom village where DIPAN DI LONG community

---

403 Article 2.

404 Colchester (n 62) 10.

405 See section 8 (2) of the 1994 Forestry Law.

forest is situated. The absence of young people in community is due to the fact that there are no schools[406] within this community which constitute some of the social amenities to be realised from the management of community forest. Article 1 (4) and 5, of the 1969 UN Convention on the Elimination of All Form of Racial Discrimination[407] provides for measures to protect indigenous ownership and control of historically occupied land and resources. The convention further stresses on the consent of indigenous people with regards to matters that may affect them. As stated by Colchester[408] the Committee on Elimination of All Forms of Racial Discrimination in its 1997 reports called on States to recognise and protect the rights of indigenous population to own, develop, control and use their communal lands, territories and resources. It further recommend that where these people have been deprived of their lands and traditionally owned territories, steps should be taken to return these lands and territories.

On the contrary in Cameroon, steps are rather being taken to completely deprive them of these lands and resources. For instance chieftaincy lands considered by communities as their only common patrimony have been classified as public property of the State,[409] completely depriving the village communities from claiming ownership. It be could argue that the assimilation of chieftaincy lands by the State is protective of such lands for as public property of the State chieftaincy lands are inalienable, imprescriptible and unattachable.[410]

The 2007 UN Declaration on the Rights of Indigenous People requires that processes which promote the recognition of the rights of indigenous people to their lands, territories and resources should be promoted. Although the declaration is not legally binding, it is an authoritative interpretation of the provisions of the International Human Rights conventions which most countries in the world continue to ignore. That is why the appropriation of forests by States is a common phenomenon around the world. It is estimated that 77% of the world's forest is owned by governments, while 95% of African forest is owned by States.[411]

[406] Interview with Yami Marie and Nubah Jean, (villagers of Nkokom) 2009.
[407] This Convention was ratified by Cameroon on the 24th of June 1971. For more on this see http://www.treaties.un.org (last consulted 7/3/2011).
[408] Colchester (n 62) 10.
[409] Article 4 (k) (1) of Ordinance no. 74/2 of 6th July 1974 to establish rules governing land tenure.
[410] Ibid section 2 (2).
[411] Cotula (n 31) 11.

5.4.2 International Labour Organsation (ILO) 169

ILO is a specialised agency of the United Nations, whose worldwide objectives are to improve labour conditions, promote productive employment and social progress, and raise living standards. It was established as an agency in 1919 by the League of Nations and still maintains that status under the UN after the Second World War in 1945.[412] Because of it concern for human standards and wellbeing, the Organisation defines international labour standards by means of conventions, which have an implication on human rights.

One of these conventions dealing with indigenous and tribal peoples' rights is ILO 169 adopted in 1989 preceded by ILO 107 adopted in 1957. ILO 169 stresses the fact that indigenous people should enjoy as much control as possible over their own economics, social and cultural development. Article 7 (1) of the convention recognises the rights of indigenous people to decide their own priorities for the process of development that affects their lives, beliefs, institutions and spiritual well-being and the land they occupy or otherwise use.

Article 13 (1) of the Convention deals with territorial rights and stipulates that "government should recognise and respect the spiritual, cultural and economic relationships that indigenous people have with their lands. Their collective rights of ownership and possession over their traditionally occupied lands should be enforced (art. 14) to guarantee local people the total control of their surroundings." Article 13 (1) of ILO 169 defines land to include "territories which covers the total environment of the area which the people concerned occupy or otherwise use."

Article 11 of ILO 107 equally recognised the collective and individual ownership by local communities of the lands they traditionally occupied. While interpreting this article in a complaint involving the tribal people of India, the ILO Committee of Experts extended local community land rights to land presently occupied irrespective of antiquity possession or occupation. The fact that the people had some form of relationship with the land even if for a short time was sufficient to form an interest.[413]

Though Cameroon is not a signatory to this convention, read together with human rights, this convention is an authoritative interpretation of the

[412] Redmond, W. A., "International Labor Organization," Microsoft® Student, Encarta 2009.

[413] Colchester (n 62) 12.

rights to property, be it individual or collective, enshrined in the Cameroon 1996 constitution earlier discussed.

5.5 Conclusion

The present land legislation in Cameroon largely influenced by colonialism does not guarantee tenure rights to local communities. The Germans through the Forestry Ordinances of 1900 and 1913 did not only monopolise the exploitation of forest resources, but classified all unoccupied land including forest land as *herrenlos Kronland* depriving local communities of any claim of ownership. This policy was adopted by the French through a Decree of March 8 1926, which classified all forests as *forêts domaniales* and placed them under the control of the French High Commissioner. Though the British recognised the rights of the local people on their customary land, English law however did not consider the forest as forming part of the customary land. The control and management of the forest was vested in the British administration.

Since independence, the legacies of these colonial administrations are still very alive in Cameroon. The 1974 land Ordinances have not only classified land into State and National lands, but have apparently abolished customary tenure rights depriving the local people of claiming ownership of community forests, a claim which is indispensable for the sustainable management of community forests.

The 1994 Forestry Law subjects the ownership of forest to land tenure not within the competence of local communities. Denial of ownership to communities in possession of community forests based on their customary land rights generate conflicts and does not augur well with the sustainable management of forests.

Customary tenure is approved by international Organisations. International Human Right Instruments such as the 1976 ICCPR, the UN Convention on the Elimination of All Forms of Racial Discrimination, the UN Convention on the Rights of the Child, the 1986 African Charter on Human and Peoples' Rights and ILO Convention 169 are all in favour of the concept. Though ILO 169 is not applicable in the Cameroon, the effective application of the above mentioned International Human Rights Instrument all ratified by Cameroon would have enforced the recognition of customary tenure and accordingly the proper management of community forests in the country. Unfortunately this is not the case.

CHAPTER SIX

ENCUMBRANCES IN INTEGRATING INDIGENOUS COMMUNITIES IN THE MANAGEMENT OF FOREST RESOURCES

6.1: Introduction

The introduction of community forests in the 1994 Forestry Law came with a lot of enthusiasm for local communities to create and manage forests, noticeable in the number of community forest application files. As of 2008, MINFOF had received about 426 community forests application files, with 177 approved simple management plans (SMP) and over 140 with signed Management Agreements.[414] Unfortunately the complicated procedure in the creation and management of these forests as will be discussed below offers opportunities for outsiders to benefit from these forests rather than the local community for whose interest the forest was intended. This chapter examines procedural difficulties faced by local communities in the creation of community forests and how outsiders benefit from this process to the detriment of the local communities concerned.

6.2: Flaws in Procedure

The procedure in the creation of community forests involve long and complicated administrative channels; it is time consuming and costly.

---

[414] See appendix 1 : *MINFOF, Fiche D'Indentification des Forest Communautaires, Situation des F.C 2008.*

6.2.1: Administrative Channel

Both the procedures for the creation and exploitation of community forests are long, not easy to be followed by local communities. This discourages communities which have embarked on creation of community forest and invites unscrupulous individuals who limit the benefits to themselves. Just like community forest management agreements, the procedure for the obtention of an exploitation title is described by local communities as very long and financially expensive. This barrier is nourished by corruption practiced along the chain. The result is that many community forests are capture by members of the local elite who provides funds and later on confiscate all the financial benefits and all the markets rights. The signing also of transportation authorisation (way bill) is also in itself, a serious barrier, as it needs the decisional involvement of many local level officials of MINFOF. Furthermore each year it is necessary to renew the certificate of exploitation in order to be able to exploit the community forest the following year. As discussed earlier, empirical evidence puts forward a series of transaction imposed by the forestry administration before signing these annual certificates. High transaction costs are also found along the value chain of the marketing of products derived from the exploitation of community forests.[415]

6.2.1.1: Long Procedure for Creating Community Forests

The creation of community forest goes through a procedure made up of the following 10 stages: village meetings to discuss community forest; formation of legal entities; identification of forest areas, consultation meeting; preparation and submission of application dossier; treatment of application dossier at the Ministry of Forestry and Wildlife, preparation of a management plan; management agreement; submission of management plan and management agreement to the local forestry officials and finally implementation of the SMP and management agreement.[416] In addition to the above cited 10 stages, the 2009 Manual provides for a provisional management agreement which is valid for a non-renewable period of two years.[417]

[415] Mbile, P. et al., "Alternate tenure and enterprise models in Cameroon: community forest in the context of community rights and forest landscape," Strategy Paper, Washington D.C, Rights and Resource Initiative, 2009.

[416] MINFOF, How to obtain a community forest, 2009.

[417] Section 5.13.1 of the 2009 Manual of the Procedure for the Attribution and Norms for the Management of Community Forests

6.2.1.2: Preparatory/Preliminary Meeting

For the initiative of creating a community forest to succeed, meetings must be organised. The first of these meetings known as the preparatory or preliminary meetings must be held before the formation of a legal entity which will be charged with the management of the community forest.[418] In the course of this meeting the population is informed of the advantages and disadvantages of each of the entities required for the management of community forests.[419] The preparatory meeting is aimed at sensitising and informing the various sectors of the community on the proposal to conserve and manage a community forest.[420]

Meetings are important to stress the participation of local communities in the management of forest resources as is the case in Peru and Scotland. In Peru for instance meetings are accompanied by a census of the community while in Scotland community forest application files are accompanied by enough signatures to demonstrate that a sufficient number of members of the local community have approved the project.[421]

Preliminary meetings may be organised by traditional authorities, other opinion leaders, local forestry officer or an accompanying structure that is actively involved in informing and sensitising the local community. Where such meetings are not organised by the administrative services, the administration must be represented at the session to advise the community. The community may hold one or several preparatory meetings.

In REPA CIG for instance 20 preliminary meetings were held, while in Tinto Living Earth organised about 72 of such meetings before convincing the local community of the necessity to create and manage a community forest. The numerous but poorly attended meetings held in these communities show the peoples' lack of interest in the project. The few members of the communities who attended meetings did so because they received incentives in the form of food and drinks.[422]

---

418 Ibid section 2.2.

419 Ibid section 3.3.

420 BHFP: Community Forestry Seminar Series. Information note 6: A process for Community Forestry in the Bamenda Highlands, November 2001 p. 2.

421 Long, C., Forest and Community control: Official process that permits formal recognition of community management and rights and their relevance to the Democratic Republic of Congo, IIED. 2010. p. 21.

422 Interview with Chief Tanyi, E. A., traditional ruler of Tinto, 2009.

6.2.1.3: Formation of Legal Entities

The preliminary meeting is followed by the formation of a legal entity which may either be EIG, CIG, Association or Co-operative Societies.[423] The formation of legal entities, for the management of community forests is also mandatory in Guatamala where associations or user groups may be formed and in Scotland where a community company with legal personality is required.[424] Unfortunately these entities are not representative of the local communities as discussed in chapter five.

The formation of modern legal entities is time consuming and follows procedures which local people are not abreast with. The 2009 Manual of Procedure for the Attribution and Norms for the Management of Community Forests provide that "the community can create more than one legal entity and that each of the legal entities can submit an application for a community forest and be granted the forest concerned."[425] This provision offers the opportunity for the creation of many entities which will compete for the attribution of the forest. The attribution of the forest to one entity and not the other will certainly create hatred and conflicts amongst the members of the competing entities which does not guarantee the sustainable management of the forest. After the formation of the legal entities a consultation meeting is held bringing together all sectors of the community.

6.2.1.4: Consultation Meeting

The second important meeting is the consultation meeting. It is described by the Forestry Decree as: "a general meeting bringing together all members of the community concerned in order to appoint an official in charge of management, define objectives and set the boundaries of the said forest."[426] This meeting is held only after the formation of the legal entity to manage the community forest. The choice of the person in charge of the legal entity to manage the forest is endorsed[427] in the course of this meeting. The meeting regroups various sectors of the community including the public services, traditional authorities, communities soliciting the forest, and their neighbours as well as elites and other support structures.

---

[423] Section 3.4 of the 2009 Manual.

[424] Long (n 8) 21.

[425] Ibid section 3.8 of the 2009 Manual.

[426] Article 28 (1) of the 1995 Forestry Decree.

[427] Section 4.1 of the 2009 Manual.

Public services here refer to MINFOF, MINEPDED, MINATD, MINADER, MINEPIA, and other administrative bodies which give advice to participant in their own area of competence, such as personnel of the Ministries of Environment, Nature protection and Sustainable Development and those in charge of Agriculture and rural development.[428] MINATD officials in their capacity as the senior authority within the area where the forest is located and as one of the signatory of the management agreement preside over the consultation meeting. These officials equally ensure that the legal entities are legally constituted and oversee that any pending disputes are resolved as far as the creation of the community forest is concerned.

MINFOF's representative acts as secretary of the consultative meeting and assist the administrative official of MINATD in the organisation of the meeting such as in drafting invitations and putting up public notices about the meeting.[429]

The presence of the neighbouring community at the consultative meeting is of great relevance. These communities are consulted for public confirmation of the boundaries proposed for the community forest. On their parts as representative of the community, the presence of traditional authorities raises the profile of the meeting. They can be useful during conflicts within the management structure on the boundary of the community forests.

The consultative meeting, being a very important step as far as the creation of community forests are concerned is chaired by the DO, SDO, Governor or Minister in charge of forestry or their representatives depending on whether the forest under consideration falls within their territorial areas of command.[430] The meeting is publicised by poster at the nearest Forestry Post, Divisional, Sub-Divisional and headquarters covered by the forests for at least forty (40) days.[431] To be more effective, it is commendable that posters be put up in the palaces of traditional rulers and why not in the compounds of their quarter heads. This nevertheless will be of relevance only to a very few number of the members of the community to read given that the level of illiteracy in forest communities

[428] Ibid section 4.2.
[429] Ibid section 4.5.
[430] Ibid sections 4.4, 4.4.1, 4.4.2 and 4.4.3.
[431] Ibid section 4.7.

cannot be doubted. Thus for information to reach the remote communities the services of town criers should be used.

Notwithstanding the importance of meetings it is alleged that some community forests such as COFAYET Bengbis discussed in chapter four was created without a consultation meeting. It is also doubtful if the creation of PREFONDE-CAMEROUN purportedly existing in Moungo Division[432] was preceded by any meeting, this is so because this forest only exists on paper. Could the non-existence of PREFONDE-CAMEROUN in the field be justified by the encumbrances faced in the creation of community forests? The creation of community forest without the consent of the local communities which ought to be obtained through preparatory and consultative meetings is clear evidence of the non-implementation of the 1992 CBD as far as the use of indigenous knowledge is concerned. Once the legal entities have been created and the consultative held, the community proceeds with the preparation and submission of the application file or dossier.

6.2.1.5: The Application File or Dossier

The application file is composed of a long list of complicated documents with financial implications provided for by article 29 (1) (a-f) of the 1995 Forestry Decree, not within the reach of local communities. These documents include:

a - A stamped application stating the objectives defined for the forest in question;

b - A situation plan of the forest, which must not exceeds five thousands (5000) hectares;

c - Documentary evidence showing the name of the community concerned as well as the address of the official appointed;

d - A description of the activities previously carried out in the forest in question;

e - The curriculum vitae of the official in charge of forestry operations;

---

[432] Informant, Mr.Wagne Echapgnmo, Divisional Delegate of Forestry and wildlife for the Moungo Division 2009.

f - The minutes of the consultative meeting in the course of which all the members of the community concerned appointed the official in charge of management, defined the objectives and boundaries of the said forest.

In addition to the above, and as mentioned earlier, the 2009 Manual also provides for a provisional management agreement.[433] The requirement of the above mentioned documents renders the process cumbersome and constitutes a draw back in the creation of community forests. Some of the above mentioned documents cannot easily be obtained by local communities. For instance the situation plan for the forest has to be drawn by the National Instituted of Cartography in Yaounde which is not within the reach of local communities. This renders the compilation of the application file difficult, serves as a disincentive to local communities and retards the creation of community forests.

That apart, the process involved in submission and evolution of the application files for the creation of community forests seems prolonged by the 2009 Manual. Unlike the 1998 Manual which required that the dossier be submitted once, the 2009 Manual provide for double submissions. That is a dossier is first submitted for the Provisional Management Agreement and the second with a SMP for the final Management Agreement.

6.2.1.6: Application for Provisional Management Agreement

Two copies of the completed file for the Provisional Management Agreement (M.A) are submitted by the local community to the local administrative official that is the Divisional Delegate who upon receiving the application issues a dated receipt to the community. The Division Delegate within 10 days of receiving the application file forwards same with justified opinion to the Regional Delegate[434] and displays a map of the area for public information.

On receiving the application file, forwarded to him by the Divisional Delegate, the Regional Delegate also forwards the said application within 10 days of it reception to the Minister in charge of Forestry. This file must be accompanied by a reasoned opinion of the Regional Delegate.[435] It is also the responsibility of the Regional Delegate to inform the competent

[433] Section 5.1 (f, g) of the 2009 Manual.
[434] Ibid section 5.7.
[435] Ibid Section 5.7.1.

administrative authority[436] of the application by a memorandum and a map of the proposed community forest.[437] More often than not the limit of 10 days is not respected by local MINFOF official (Divisional and Regional Delegates), and retards the creation of community forests.

If the forest in question is not covered by a logging title or does not encroach on the permanent forest estate, then the provisional management agreement is signed by the Minister in charge of Forestry.[438] If the application file is rejected, the central administration in charge of forestry drafts a letter stating clearly the reasons for the rejection. The letter is transmitted to the community concerned together with the two copies of the application file via the Regional Delegate.[439] The community corrects the error stated in the rejection letter and resubmits the application for approval.

If the central administration in charge of forestry does not receive the application file sixty days from its initial submission to the Divisional Delegate, the community reserves the right to submit a copy of the file together with the submission receipts to the Minister in charge of Forestry. Upon reception, the Minster has 15 working days to reply the community concerned, failing which the application will be deemed granted.[440]

The provisional management agreement is valid for a non-renewable period of two years.[441] As soon as it is approved or considered granted, the community may start carrying out the planned forest operations. By the end of the provisional management agreement, the community has to prepare and submit a SMP for a final Management Agreement. As stated earlier the above procedures are fraud with administrative bottlenecks and corruption.

6.2.1.7: Preparation of Simple Management Plan and Final Management Agreement

A simple management plan is required as one of the constitutive document for the creation of community forests and the process of its

[436] This may be the SDO if the forest in question is located within a Division or the Governor if the forest spans two or more Divisions of the Region.
[437] Section 3.2.7 of the 1998 Manual.
[438] Ibid section 5.13.
[439] Ibid section 5.14.
[440] Ibid section 5.12.
[441] Ibid section 5.13.1.

preparation is long. For instance the stages involved in the preparation of the SMP include discussions with members of the community stressing on the importance and different aspects of the plan. Members are selected and trained on issues such as, interviewing, surveying and map drawing techniques. The training is followed by village and forest surveys, to collect data necessary for the preparation of the SMP. As stated by some authors these surveys permit the community to demarcate recognised and acceptable boundaries of the community forest.[442] The data collected are analysed with a view of preparing the five years plan of action and the annual operation plan which are presented to the local community for approval before being submitted to local MINFOF official for transmission to MINFOF.

The content of the SMP has been increased from five chapters in the 1998 Manual to eight in the 2009 Manual. A remarkable innovation is found in chapter seven of the 2009 Manual which deals with planning of resources and revenue management activities, guiding communities on the management of income derived from forest exploitation.

Examining the content of the plan which differs from one community to the other, coupled with the difficulties involved in its elaboration one wonders why the law refers to it as "simple" for it is not in actual fact simple, considering that section 6.1.3 of the 2009 Manual requires the following document to be appended to a SMP:

- A copy of the letter of Provisional Management Agreement;
- Full inventory report of the five years compartment;
- Report of participatory prospecting;
- Report of the socio- economic and environmental survey;
- Certificate of surface area measurement;
- Articles of Association and By-laws of legal entity;
- Minutes of consultative meeting
- Minutes of constituent General Assembly;
- Curriculum vitae of person in charge of forest operations;
- Registration certificate or declaration of receipt of the legal entity.

The long procedure and the technicalities involved in the elaboration of the SMP and the numerous documents required for it approval

---

442 Mortier, P. et al., Delimitation of Community Forest, CFDP, Yaounde, 2003, p. 10.

constitute a major drawback in the participation of local communities in the management of forest resources through community forests.

From the foregoing it will be noticed that guidelines and technical methodologies in the preparation of a SMP are imposed by forestry officials, without taking into account local values, community representations of forested landscapes and local or indigenous knowledge.

6.2.1.8: Submission of SMP and Final Management Agreement

Seven copies of the SMP and Final Management Agreements are prepared by the community with the assistance of local forestry officials. The community conserves one copy and submits six to the Divisional Delegate who issues them a dated receipt.[443] The latter forwards the six copies of the plan and agreement to the Regional Delegate with his reasoned recommendation. The Regional Delegate checks the SMP and Final Management Agreement and forwards same with his reasoned opinion to the Minister in charge of forestry.

If the SMP is rejected by the Minister of Forestry and Wildlife, it is sent back to the community with reasons for it rejection for correction or modification to be made. The forest in question is then reserved for twenty four (24) additional months as from the date of it rejection awaiting the community to resubmit the application.[444]

Upon approval of the SMP, the Minister sends six copies to the Regional Delegate to be forwarded to the competent administrative authority (Governor, SDO) who must sign the management agreement within 15 days of it reception. The law is silent as to what happens if the agreement is not signed within the above mentioned 15 days.

After signing the management agreement, the competent administrative authority conserves a copy and return five copies to the Divisional Delegate for distribution. Copies are sent to the community concerned, the chief of forestry post within whose jurisdiction the forest is located, the Regional Delegate and the Minister of forestry and Wildlife following the same channel that was used to have it signed.

---

[443] Section 6.4.1 of the 2009 Manual.

[444] Ibid section 6.4.4.2.

If the community does not receive a reply within sixty days from the date of the initial submission of the application file to the Divisional Delegate, the community reserves the right to submit against a receipt a copy of the SMP and final Management Agreement directly to the service in charge of community forestry at MINFOF together with the relevant receipt.[445]

The final Management Agreement is considered the birth certificate of a community forest. Once legalised it constitutes the final stage in the creation of the community forest and marks the beginning of the execution of the SMP. Notwithstanding this agreement, the community has to go through another long and complicated procedure before exploiting the forest.

6.2.2: Exploitation Procedure

As discussed earlier in chapter seven, the procedure followed between the signing of the management agreement and the exploitation of the forest is long and discouraging to the local communities. For instance before embarking on the exploitation of community forests the community must have carried out an exploitation inventory as well as an Environmental Impact Assessment (EIA) which are costly and requires a lot of technicalities. In addition the local community has to respect the preliminary requirements for exploitation such as providing an annual plan of operation, annual certificates of exploitation, notification of commencement of activity and annual reports. Though intended to enhance control by the forestry administration, these reports are hardly produced may be due to administrative bottleneck involved in the process.

The exploitation of timber is subjected to titles such as sale of standing volume, forest exploitation permits and individual felling authorisations which are not easy to obtain by local communities. In India for instance under JFM in one State, ten different permits were required for a community to be able to sell its timber.[446] It was difficult to determine or distinguish the different types of exploitation titles to which some community forests such as REPA CIG and NDECUDA were subjected. Also the irregular, delay and sometimes non deliverance of Way Bills for

---

445 Ibid section 6.4.5.

446 Scherr, S. J., White & D. Kaimowitz, "Making Markets work for Forest Communitie," Policy Brief, Forest trend, Washington D.C, 2000.

transportation of products constitute obstacles in the exploitation and commercialisation of community forests products.

The long administrative channel required for the creation and exploitation of community forest not withstanding, the treatment of the application file may take as long as nine years as was the case of CADBAP community forest in the East Region. For example the initiative to create this community forest started in 1999. In 2001 the Association charged with the management of this forest was created. An application file was compiled and submitted. The forest was reserved for the community in 2002[447] and the management agreement signed in 2008.

6.2.2.1: Financial Cost

The creation of community forest is constrained with administrative bottlenecks and corruption. The procedure is long, complicated and very costly requiring about 16 million or more for it realisation.[448] Fomete states that the cost of compiling an application file and following through the process varies between 200.000 FCFA and 1.050.000 FCFA. The cost of drawing up a SMP varies between 1.200.000 FCFA and 14.000.000 FCFA in the case of community forest measuring 3.500 hectares.[449] Some of the activities involved in the process are activities which cannot conveniently be financed by village communities without clear sources of income making way for intruders. This includes the holding of meetings; formation of legal entities; preparation and submission of application dossiers; preparation of management plan; environmental impact assessment; various costs of transportation and the like.

Difficulties faced by local communities to raise the money required offers opportunity for financially powerful elites to provide the money and subsequently become de facto owners or beneficiaries of community forests.[450] This was precisely the case with REPA CIG, NDECUDA and COFAYET discussed in chapter four.

---

[447] See reservation Order no 0094/FR/MINEF/SG/DF/CFC/CE.

[448] Ngwasiri, C. N., "The Community Forestry Program in Cameroon: A Participatory Management Option? CIFOR, Working paper no. 5, Yaounde, 2000, p. 21.

[449] Fomete, T., "Cost of acquiring a community forest and profitability of community forest exploitation alternative," in MINEF, "The Setting Up of Community Forests in Cameroon, Report on the Forum for the Sharing of Field Experience," Nguelemendouka, 14-17 November, 2000, p. 12.

[450] Interview with Mrs Mokom Mangwi , FMO Baba II community forest, 2009.

6.3: Incursion by Legal Entities

The legal entities (Associations, EIG, CIG and Cooperative Societies) charged with the management of community forest could be considered as intruders as discussed in chapter four. They do not represent local communities as far as membership is concerned nor use indigenous technologies and practices in the management of community forest as demanded in article 8 (j) of the 1992 CBD.

Considered as intruders, legal entities manage the forest not for the welfare of the community but for their private and selfish interest. For instance GIC DIPAN DI LONG is managed by an FMO who resides in Douala and hardly visits the village. Most of the projects conceived in the simple management plan of this forest were not realised, as the funds earmarked for the projects were embezzled. The offenders are not accountable because they are not answerable to local communities which do not only lack the means but are ignorant of the content of their annual reports. For instance, about 90% of members of the local community contacted during our field work were ignorant of the proceeds made from community forests, let alone know how they were spent.

In some communities, legal entities constitute a threat to local Institutions and in most cases lead to conflict. This is the case with GIC JAGBRA, Laikom, Mindourou and Zoalabo II communities where the indigenous institution (village Council, Fon) are struggling to take over the management of the community forests from the legal entities. In Laikom for instance the Fon finds it difficult to understand why the management of a forest owned by the village should be handed to a different person other than the customary custodian of the forest, who is the Fon. He thinks that government decision in the management of community forest is misdirected. In Zoalabo II, trees felled without the authorization of traditional authorities were said to have been mysteriously destroyed.[451]

6.3.1: Hidden Agendas of Elites

Elites may exert either positive or negative influence towards the creation and management of community forests, since they are considered as the "eyes of the community." Elites who are well versed with the concept of community forests may sensitise local communities on the needs and

[451] Interview with Mr. Edourou Vital, Coordinator of PERAD in Lomie Sub-Division, 2009.

importance of having and managing community forests. On the contrary elites who are not well informed about the concept may anti-sensitise local people thus making the idea unacceptable by local communities.[452]

Generally, as far as forest management is concerned elites attached themselves more with the administration than local communities. The local communities generally consider these elites as accomplices of the administration in the management of forest resources.[453] Most often they do not defend the interest of local communities and have hidden and selfish intention and use community forest to cover their illegal exploitation of the forest. Elite's incursion is not peculiar to Cameroon. Due to the complex process of obtaining a community forest in Latin America, only communities with outside supports are able to obtain forests and open up the threat of elites capture.

Most elites took advantage of the cumbersome procedure in the creation of community forest as channels for obtaining portions of the forest[454] and manage them as their "private property."[455] Most elites are share holders in exploitation companies and exploit the forest without respecting the SMP paving the way for forest degradation. A Clear example is the case of REPA CIG financed single-handedly by an elite with the sum of approximately 15 million FCFA,[456] with the understanding that the creditor was to exploit the forest until he recovers his money before handing over the exploitation to the community. From the 2008 Annual report of activities of this community forest, closed to 25 million FCFA was generated. This implies that the exploiter ought to have recovered his money and consequently handed over the excess and management of the forest to the local community. Unfortunately this is not the case. This situation has made the local community to have a negative perception of

452 Nkwatoh, A., "Korup Project and Community Forest: The Race and Bridges on the Way" in Community Forestry Network no. 005, Yaounde, 2001, p. 10.

453 Bigombe, P. L and Nkoum-Me-Ntseng, L.M.M., « Vers la Décentralisation de la Gestion Forestière au Cameroun? Dynamique de Contestation de l'Etat Forestière et de Construction de la Gestion Participative des Ressources Forestière » in Bulletin Arbres, Forêts et Communautés Rurales, no. 15/16, Spécial Cameroun, 1998, p. 9.

454 Fonkem, S. N., "Rape of the Forest: Sacrificing Trees for Wood" in Insight Magazine, no. 003, CIM, Cameroon, 2003, p. 21.

455 Auzel, P.H and Nchoji, N., « La Foresterie Communautaire dans le Sud Cameroun. Etat et Processus, Acteurs Impliqués et Perspectives, » DFID, BHC Yaounde, 2000, p. 7.

456 We consider it an estimate because Mr. Asoe Kingsley who is resident in the village and actually doing the work of the FMO talked of 20 million, while the FMO himself, son of the creditor talked of 15 million. The FMO was unwilling to show us the documentary evidence of this financial transaction.

the role of elites whose knowledge of the Forestry Law gives them advantage over the local communities. This state of affairs renders decentralisation in forest management informal and fragmented.[457]

6.4: Corrupt Practices of Administrative Officials

The illegal and dishonest use of power by public officials and dedicated public service to enrich themselves often referred to as corruption constitute a canker worm that affect the effective creation and exploitation of community forests in Cameroon. Corruption which could take various forms such as bribery and embezzlement is not only one of the causes for difficulties faced in the creation and exploitation of community forests, but equally for the non-enforcement of policies, injustice, poverty, want of good governance and the formulation of biased policies.[458] Though it is difficult to prove the existence of corrupt practices since corruption often takes the form of black marketing, the existence of a project to fights against corruption in schools (*Projet FACTS*)[459] and an anti- corruption commission in Cameroon and other African country such as Gabon and Central African Republic confirms the existence of corrupt practices in these countries. Transparency International, a global coalition formed to fight corruption rated Cameroon as the most corrupt country in 1998 and 1999.

Corruption in Cameroon has eaten into the fabric of the society so much that the administration takes advantage of the long and complicated procedure in the creation and exploitation of community forests to exploit local communities. For instance and as mentioned above, the creation of community forests follows a long and expensive procedure which is hardly completed by the local communities. Elites therefore collude with the administration and create these forests without the consent of the local communities. This was precisely the case of COFAYET Bengbis created without preliminary meetings and managed by an entity unilaterally formed by the exploiter. If not through corruption, how can one explain

[457] Oyono, P. R., "Forest Management, Systemic Crisis and Policy Change: Socio-Organisational Roots of Ecological Uncertainties in the Cameroon's Decentralisation Model," CIFOR 2002, Paper prepared for World Resource Institute (WRI) Workshop on "Decentralisation and the Environment," Bellagio, Italy, 2002, p. 2.

[458] Nchunu, S., "The Sustainable use of Forest and Wildlife Resources in Central Africa: Key Policy Challenges" in Musiti, B.W., (ed.) Second Pan-African Symposium on the Sustainable use of Natural Resources in Africa, IUCN, 2003, p. 227.

[459] See generally "Generations Integres" Magasine of information and Education, No.002, January-February 2011.

the fact that some community forests are purported to be existing only on papers,[460] whereas the initiative to create these forest ought to originate from local communities.

The corrupt practice of administrative official even extends to the exploitation of the forest. As discussed in chapter six, most of the preliminary requirements for exploitation are not respected and government seems not to be disturbed. Annual reports which are the principal documents required by government to control the exploitation of community forests are hardly presented by the local communities. For instance CADBAP and GIC JAGRA C.F have never submitted annual reports. For close to eight years of theirs existence, we could only trace one and two annual reports for Tinto Clan and BBNRMC C.F community forests respectively.

Lack of control by administrative officials, which could guide, correct and sanction communities for non-respect of SMP are not carried out and constitute shortcomings in the sustainable management of community forests. The absence of administrative control can be justified by corrupt practices, as was the case of GIC DIPAN DI LONG, where despite the non-respect of the SMP, annual reports were prepared without the knowledge of the local community and the SMP renewed without their consent. The laxity of the forestry administration in controlling and sanctioning community forest legal entities for the non-respect of community forest SMPs is indicative that government is not willing to ensure effective community participation in forest management as required by the 1992 CBD.

6.5: Conclusion

Since independence, government has been involved in numerous reforms aimed at improving the management of forest and environmental resources. These reforms reached it peak in 1994 with the introduction of the concept of community forests aimed at incorporating local communities in the management of forest resources close to their settlements with the aim of improving their living standards as well as ensuring resource sustainability.

---

460 This is for instance the case of PREFONDE - Cameroon purported to be found within the Moungo Division.

The realisation of this project is faced with a lot of encumbrances which discourage local communities. For instance, the administrative channels to be followed and procedure for exploitation of community forests are long and costly. The communities have to organise preparatory and consultation meetings, form legal entities, prepare, submit and follow the evolution of application files for provisional management agreements, SMP and final management agreements.

The procedure for the exploitation of community forests is equally long, costly, complicated and opens avenues for intruders such as legal entities and elites who embezzle benefits intended for local communities. The administration equally takes advantage of this long and complicated procedure in the creation and exploitation of community forests to carry out corrupt practices which are detrimental to both local communities and forest conservation.

CHAPTER SEVEN

GENERAL CONCLUSION

7.1: Moving Forward: Enhancing the Integration of Indigenous Communities in the Management of Environmental Resources

To ensure effective integration of local communities in the management of natural resources as recommended by national and international laws, some institutional and organisational reforms are indispensable.

72: Institutional Reforms

Modern institutions for the integration of indigenous communities in the management of environmental resources need to be actual representative of local communities. Also local institutions and customary land tenure rights should be legally recognised. Communities' property rights over natural resources should be recognized. Natural resource management plans such as Simple Management Plans of community forests should take into consideration the sustainable management of intangible as well as the tangible benefits of the forests.

Existing local institutions such as chiefdoms, sacred societies and community user groups that have direct link with the natural resources and its management should be recognised, strengthened and empowered as significant contributors in sustainable resource management. This is precisely what obtains in Tanzania where decisions concerning forest management are taken at village council levels,[461] representing local communities. In order to have a legal entity that is representative of the indigenous community, government could restructure existing local organisations such as traditional councils, village development committees

---

[461] Long, C., Forest and Community control: Official process that permits formal recognition of community management and rights and their relevance to the Democratic Republic of Congo, IIED, 2010, p. 13.

or unions and give them legal status, that is, by transforming traditional legitimacy into legal legitimacy,"[462] as was the case with traditional or village chiefdoms. The law provides that:

> All traditional chieftaincies are placed under the authority of chiefs, assisted by councils of elders, the constitution of which is determined by local tradition.[463]

An example is the legal recognition of existing local communities' institutions in Peru[464] which involves invariably the recognition of traditional natural resource-related knowledge embedded in these institutions. Local communities have since time immemorial used this knowledge to manage resources such as forests. In some local communities like in Oku village, forest user groups such as carvers, hunters, honey farmers, traditional medicine gatherers, women and youths exist. These groups are endowed with considerable indigenous knowledge and practices as a result of their long relationship with the forest.[465] In these groups the leaders are democratically elected and represent the people, hence have the mandate to sanction offences.

The recognition of indigenous institutions will also legitimize indigenous system of sanctions for violation of both modern and customary rules that apply to natural resources. Customary sanctions that will complement statutory sanctions are commendable in regulating and controlling illegal exploitation of natural resources. This is because local communities attach a lot of respect to customary rules for fear of the calamity that may befall defaulters. In Ivory Coast for instance, it is believed by the Aouan people that over-exploitation of trees and the cultivation of over-steep slops would call forth *Assie*, a female matrilineal deity who is dangerous to humans.[466] Even threats from traditional

---

462 Egbe, S. E., "The concept of Community Forestry under Cameroonian Law" in Journal of African Law, 45, vol. 1, UK, 2001, p. 46.

463 Our translation, see article 6 of Decree No. 77/245 of July 1977 on the Organisation of Chieftaicy. The original text in French reads "*Toute chefferie traditionnelle est placée sous l'autorité d'un chef, assisté d'un conseil de notable, formé selon la tradition locale.*"

464 Long (n 19) 21.

465 Okafor, J., "The Use of Farmer Knowledge in Non-Wood Forest Product Research" in Non-Wood Forest Products of Central Africa. Current Research Issues and Prospects for Conservation and Development, FAO, 1999, p. 123.

466 FAO, Common Forest Resource Management. Annoted Bibliography of Asia, Africa, and Latin America, FTP-FAO, Rome, 1993, p. 109.

authorities also have a lot of influence in the conservation of forest and tree resources. The Hausa Sultans of Zinder in Niger threatened to decapitate anyone who fells a *Faidherbia Albida* tree and to amputate the arm of anyone who mutilates a tree of this specie.[467] Indigenous communities fear customary and spiritual sanctions which though not codified are more effective than State-enacted sanctions; hence need to be legally recognised.

7.2.1: Recognition of Customary Collective Rights

The integration of indigenous communities in the management of natural resources is weakened by the fact that, ownership of these resources is subject to land ownership which gives preference to statutory as against customary tenure. For local communities to effectively participate in the management of natural resources, a reform which grants collective or communal land title to indigenous communities should be adopted. This will be similar to what obtains in Papua New Guinea, (PNG) Uganda, Tanzanian, Scotland and India as well as in Cambodia, Venezuela and Canada.

In Cambodia "collective ownership of land by local community is recognised and includes all the rights and protection of ownership as are enjoyed by private owners. The local community does not have the right to dispose of any collective ownership to any person or group."[468] The 1999 Constitution of Venezuela recognises the rights of indigenous communities to their land and habitat as "inalienable, un-leasable, un-mortgageable, un transferable collective property." In this country, local communities' lands are clearly demarcated with officially recognised boundaries. The recognition and enforcement of collective title is based on the occupation of land by indigenous communities considered as proof of possession. As affirmed by the Canadian Supreme Court, in *Calder v. Attorney General of British Columbia (1973)*, possession is of itself proof of ownership. Possession is considered as 9/10[469] of the law and cannot be determined arbitrarily. A similar position could be adopted for indigenous communities in Cameroon. The recognition of customary collective tenure confers on the community, ownership and use in perpetuity and gives them long term security over natural

---

467 Ibid.

468 cf. Chi (n14) 28.

469 This implies that the person in possession is protected by the law. He enjoys all the right of ownership except the right of disposal.

resources as opposed to what obtains for instance with community forests rights whereby, the duration is for a limited period of 25 years as per the agreement.[470]

The absence of recognition of customary tenure does not give security to land, negatively influences the proper management of natural resources and weakens the ability of indigenous communities to defend their interest against companies that seek to exploit their resources. This was the case in *Kimbi Moses Ndoh V. Groupement D'Entreprise Trapp-Strabag Belfinger + Berger.*[471] In that case the Wum High Court held that the Mejang village community had no basis on which to claim damages for trespass and destruction of resources on their customary land against a German construction company, because the land and resources were considered State property. A similar decision was arrived at by the Kumbo High court in *Amidou Lukong V. Razel Road Construction Company Ltd.*[472] In this case the defendant exploited quarries on land in the plaintiff's possession in Bui Division of the North-West Region. The plaintiff was never compensated for the exploitation and destruction, and sued the defendant for trespass and conversion. The High Court of Bui decided against the plaintiff and held that without a land certificate the land was national land and subject to State management. The legal implications of the above cases will remain the same to serve as precedents in the management other natural resources.

7.2.2: Community Property Rights as Private Individual Right

To ensure the integration of indigenous communities in the sustainable management of natural resources, the property rights of local communities over these resources should be recognised. For instance, the 1948 Universal Declaration of Human Rights recognises the rights of everyone to own property individually as well as in association with others.[473] The recognition of property rights of local communities is also echoed in the 2007 United Nation Declaration on the Rights of Indigenous People that calls on States to legally recognise and protect indigenous territories and resources.[474] The declaration recognises the rights of local

---

[470] Nain, B. E., "Participatory Forest Management A Strategy for the Sustainable Management of African Forests: Some Experience from Cameroon," CFU /CFDP/DF/MINEF, Yaounde, 1999, p. 7.

[471] WHC/2/98 (unreported).

[472] HCK/5/95 (unreported).

[473] Article 17

[474] See article 26 (1) of the UN GA resolution 61/295.

communities to own, use, develop and control the land, territories and resources they possess by reason of traditional ownership and other traditional occupation or use.[475]

Since natural resources in Cameroon constitute State property, it is commendable that at the expiration of some management agreements such as forest management agreements, government should return the resources to the local communities recognising their property rights. Such recognition will confer on the communities the right to manage the resources for an undetermined duration and pay taxes[476] to the State, just as any private operator. In Gambia, though there is an agreement between the community and the State, the terms of the agreement confers permanent ownership rights of resources to the community, a right which can only be revoked through a legal process if there is serious mismanagement by community.[477]

7.2.3: Conservation of Intangible and Tangible Benefits

The benefits derived from sustainable management of natural resources such as forest are both tangible and intangible and are inherently interlinked. Forests simple management plans (SMPs) lay emphasize only on management of tangible products whereas natural resources such as forests provide services which are intangible such as hydrology, soil protection and global climate regulation. Thus the integration of indigenous community in the management of natural resources will not only enhance the sustainability of tangible benefits but also the intangible values of natural resources.

7.3: Organisational and Logistic Reforms

The procedure and cost involved for integrating indigenous communities in the management of natural resources should be affordable.

7.3.1: Processing of Management Agreement

The integration of local communities in the management of resources such as forests follows a long and complicated procedure starting

---

475 Ibid article 26 (2).

476 In Gambia the community pay 15% of their income as taxes to the State.

477 Long (n 19) 13.

from the local to the central administration. For effective participation of local communities in the creation of these forests, application files should be endorsed by recognised local authorities such as traditional chiefs or fons, thus taking advantage of the current decentralisation process in the country. For instance in Gambia before a community management agreement is signed an attestation from the traditional chief who has customarily ownership of the land must be presented.[478] Such a policy will spare the community from the intervention of intruders and corrupt practices by outsiders. It will also limit the intervention of elites who have hidden agendas and benefit from proceeds to the detriment of local communities.

7.3.2: Controls

The absence or irregularity of control of by the government constitutes some of the reasons for the poor management of natural resources. MINFOF should assume and enforce its field controls in addition to ensuring that field reports on management of natural resources are timely. These reports should be controlled, followed by periodic field visits as provided for regulations.[479] To render this feasible, government should educate and empower indigenous communities, train and employ more workers to increase and strengthen government field staff who are generally poorly equipped both technically and logistically.[480]

7.3.3: Cost of Application Files for the Management of Some Natural Resources

The cost of acquiring the right to co-manage some resources such as a forest varies considerably, depending on whether the community concerned employs the services of Service Providers, uses technical assistance from MINFOF or carries out most of the activities themselves. The cost of compiling an application file and follow up through the hierarchy for approval varies between 200,000 FCFA and 1,050,000 FCFA, while the cost of drawing up a SMP is between 1000 FCFA

---

478 Long, (n 19) 13.

479 See section 8.2.2 of in the 2009 manual of procedure and norms for the management of community forests.

480 Mbaelele, M. M et Rioust, A. L., « Investissement en Biodiversité et en Protection des Zones Forestières du Zaïre » in Cleaver, K. et al. (eds.) Conservation of West and central African Rainforest, WBEP, no. 1. Washington D.C USA, 1992, p. 34.

and 4000 FCFA[481] per hectare, usually not affordable to indigenous communities.

Is commendable that, government should sponsor a good percentage of the above cost, and we dare suggest 75-80%. This could be done either by awarding some grants or subventions or even loans to the community concerned. Modalities of repayment should be laid down to commence when the community starts generating income from the management of the resource. This will protect the community from selfish and greedy elites or individuals who invest huge sums of money to assist the community and end up transforming the project into "personal businesses."

7.4: Conclusion

As confirmed by this study, local communities had since time immemorial managed environmental resources on which their very existence is based. Colonialism replaced indigenous management systems and institutions with State or modern systems which favoured the exploitation than conservation of natural resources. Faced with internal and external demands for the integration of indigenous communities in the management of natural resources, government developed legal and institutional frameworks for resource management to reflect the integration of indigenous communities.

National legal and institutional frameworks that were developed to implement the 1992 Convention on Biological Diversity (CBD) are found in pieces of legislations, enforced by the government represented by MINFOF. Examples of national enactments include the 1996 Constitution which requires the participation of all citizens in the protection of the environment;[482] the 1994 Forestry Law which paved the way for the introduction of community forest in the country;[483] the 1996 Environment Law which calls for the participation of local communities in environmental management;[484] and a variety of customary laws applicable by virtue of section 27 of the Southern Cameroons High Court Law (SCHCL) 1955,

[481] Fomete, T., "Cost of acquiring a community forest and profitability of community forest exploitation alternative," in MINEF, "The Setting Up of Community Forests in Cameroon, Report on the Forum for the Sharing of Field Experience," Nguelemendouka, 14-17 November, 2000, p. 12.

[482] See preamble of Law no. 96/06 of 18 January 1996 amending the 1972 Constitution.

[483] See articles 37 & 38 of the 1994 Forestry Law.

[484] Article 3 of the 1996 Environmental Law.

which promoted the use of indigenous knowledge and practices in the management of natural resources.

Internationally, "hard" and "soft" law instruments have been adopted promoting the integration of indigenous communities in the management of natural resources. "Hard" law instruments include: the 1968 African Convention on Nature and Natural Resources; the 1992 Convention on Climate change which calls on States to promote and facilitate public participation in addressing climate change and its effects;[485] the 2003 Maputo Convention on Nature and Natural Resources[486] and the 2005 COMIFAC Treaty,[487] both calling on contracting States to ensure the participation of indigenous communities in the management of natural resources. "Soft" laws instruments include 1972 Stockholm Declaration[488] and the 1999 Yaounde Declaration encouraging the participation of local communities in the sustainable management of environmental resources.

Beside legal framework are State and traditional institutions promoting the integration of local communities in the management of natural resources. The principal State institution promoting this initiative is the Ministry of Forestry and Wildlife. This ministerial department is expected to work in synergy with other related ministries such as the Ministry of Environment and Nature Protection (MINEP), Ministry of Agriculture and Rural Development (MINAGRI), Ministry of Scientific Research and Innovation (MINRESI) and the Ministry of Higher Education (MINSUP).

Regarding traditional institutions it was found that fondoms or chieftaincies, village traditional councils and quarter heads were involved at various levels in mobilising the participation of local communities in natural resource management.

Though these traditional institutions use indigenous knowledge and practices for natural resources management their customary land rights needed legal recognition. For instance, ownership of forestland constitutes an incentive for local communities to participate in sustainable management of forests resources. Unfortunately colonial policies deprived

---

485 Article 6 (a) (iii) of the 1992 Convention on Climate Change.

486 Article xvii of the 2003 Maputo Convention.

487 Article 1 of 2005 COMIFAC Treaty.

488 See principle 4 of the 1972 Stockholm Declaration.

local community of land and forest rights. For example in Francophone Cameroon, the French Colonial Administration through a Decree of March 8 1926 classified all forests as *forêts domaniales*. These colonialists adopted the German policy of deprivation and declared all unoccupied and unexploited lands as vacant and placed them under the control of French High Commissioner, depriving local communities of their ancestral lands and customary ownership. On their part, the British in Anglophone Cameroon did not consider forest as constituting part of the land, depriving local communities from claiming rights over such resources.

This colonial policy of deprivation was adopted by the present 1974 land legislation which gives preference to statutory as against customary land tenure which is indispensable in the sustainable management of natural resources. The 1974 land ordinances abolished the concept of community land and forest, militated against community ownership and customary tenure.

The disrespect of customary tenure is contrary to the provisions of International Human Rights Instruments such as the 1966 International Covenant on Civil and Political Rights (ICCPR) which acknowledges local peoples' rights to freely pursue their economic, social and cultural development;[489] the UN 1969 Convention on the Elimination of All Forms of Racial Discrimination which provides measures to protect indigenous ownership and control of historically occupied land and resources;[490] the 1989 UN Convention on the Rights of the Child which recognises the rights of local communities to own and manage their ancestral lands;[491] the 1986 African Charter on Human and Peoples' Rights which guarantees the rights to property and stipulates that this rights "may only be encroached upon in the general interest of the community and in accordance with the provisions of appropriate laws."[492] International Labour Organsation (ILO) 169 also calls for the recognition and respect of indigenous collective rights of ownership over traditionally occupied lands.[493]

---

489 Article 1 of the 1976 International Convention on Civil and Political Rights (ICCPR).

490 Article 1 (4) and 5, of the 1969 UN Convention on the Elimination of All Form of Racial Discrimination.

491 Article 30 of 1989 UN Convention on the Rights of the Child protects cultural rights in case of indigenous children and by implication indigenous people as a whole.

492 Article 14 the 1986 African Charter on Human and Peoples' Rights.

493 Articles 13 (1) and (14) of ILO 169.

With the exception of ILO 169, the above human rights instruments have been ratified by Cameroon, hence the need for their effective implementation and enforcement.

Natural resources such as forests provide a wide range of tangible and intangible benefits. As tangible benefits, the forest provides wood and non-timber forest products. It equally serves as habitat for both human beings and animals and constitutes a source of income to local communities and government. Intangible benefits are related to the ecologically functions of the forest and can only be realised if the forest is conserved or subjected to limited human intervention. Ecologically forest controls erosion, influences water availability and mitigates the adverse effect of climate change, let alone its importance for indigenous cultural practices and religious worships.[494]

Considering the above mentioned importance of forest it is commendable that the 1994 Forestry Law and Simple Management Plans (SMPs) of community forests should provide for the protection of tangible and intangible benefits given that article v (1) of the 2003 Maputo convention define renewable resources to include tangible and intangible resources which include soil, water, flora and fauna as well as non-renewable resources.

The sustainability of natural resources can only be assured if the right stakeholders are involve in its management. Two principal stakeholders (government and indigenous community) are legally involved in the creation and management of natural resources in community forests.[495] Government is represented by MINFOF and local community by modern legal entities which may be (Associations, Common Initiative Groups (CIG) Economic Interest Groups (EIG) and Cooperative Societies). A comparative study of the objectives, location and creation of indigenous institutions vis-à-vis modern legal entities revealed that the use of modern legal entities constituted some of the reasons for the ineffective management of natural resources because this was not in conformity with provisions of the 1992 CBD that advocate the use of local institutions endowed with indigenous knowledge and practices in the management of natural resources.[496]

[494] Chi, M. A., " Legal recognition of sacred forests in Cameroon: Giving customary communal ownership rights statutory tenure rights," in Bojang, F. et al (eds) Natural Resource Tenure Systems and their Implication for Agriculture, Food security and Nature conservation in Africa, Nature and Faune, vol. 24. Issue 2, FAO, 2010, p. 26.

[495] See section 37 (1) of the 1994 Forestry Law and article 3 (11) of the 1995 Forestry Decree.

[496] See article 8 (j) of the 1992 CBD.

In practice indigenous institutions ought to be located within local communities, headed by traditional rulers, existed since time immemorial and are endowed with indigenous knowledge necessary for the effective management of natural resources. In some sectors, indigenous institutions have the mandate to enforce regulations relating to the use of some natural resources.[497] Modern legal entities such as Associations, Common Initiative Groups (CIG) Economic Interest Groups (EIG) and Cooperative Societies were indiscriminately created in rural and urban areas in the early 90s, to ameliorate the economic situation of their members. Their objectives are incompatible with sustainable management of natural resources in general and forest in particular.

It was established that the integration of indigenous communities in the management of natural resources faces lots of encumbrances. For instance for the procedure of integrating local communities in the management of forest resources is long, complicated costly and consequently weakens the enthusiasm of indigenous communities to manage natural resources.. Because local communities hardly meet up with these requirements, intruders such as elites, natural resource exploiters and the administration take advantage of the situation for selfish interests.

[497] Article 93 of the 1996 Environmental Law; See also section 142 of the 1994 Forestry law which provides that before forestry official search houses within the community to detect criminals, they must consult traditional authorities.